Flying Stories

Flying Stories

By John M. Miller

*A chronicle of aviation history
from Jennys to jets
by the pilot who flew through it all*

COMPILED BY THE AMERICAN BONANZA SOCIETY AIR SAFETY FOUNDATION

©2002 by the American Bonanza Society
Air Safety Foundation

First Edition

Published in the United States by the American Bonanza Society/Air Safety
Foundation, a nonprofit organization dedicated to the development of aviation
educational and safety programs and materials. Proceeds from the sale of this book
go to the Endowment Fund of the ABS Air Safety Foundation.

The American Bonanza Society is an international private pilots' association whose
strength comes from the participation and enthusiasm of its more than 10,000
members who are owners, operators and enthusiasts of Beech Bonanza-type airplanes.

The stories in this book have been previously published in the *ABS Magazine*,
a monthly publication of the American Bonanza Society, Inc.

Edited by Nancy Johnson, ABS Executive Director, and
Betty Rowley, Patric Rowley & Partners, Wichita, Kansas.
Cover and interior design by Jim Simpson, Simpson Design, Wichita, Kansas.
Consultant, Patric Rowley, Wichita, Kansas.

Information regarding the Society is available on the ABS website
<www.bonanza.org> or by contacting ABS Headquarters, P.O. Box 12888,
Wichita, Kansas 67277. Phone 316-945-1700.

Printed by Village Press, Traverse City, Michigan, U.S.A.

ISBN 0-9722073-0-9

The American Bonanza Society
invited me to share with fellow members my experiences as a pilot.
This book is a collection of stories I've written
over the last several years, published in the ABS Magazine.
Although my original "audience" was pilots, there is plenty of history
and excitement for the nonaviation reader as well.
I hope you enjoy them—JMM

John Miller (center) with his Standard J-1, his brother Erik and mother Florence.
Phtoto taken at Dickerson's Field in Poughkeepsie, New York, June 8, 1928.

Preface

I soloed in 1923 in a Jenny, graduated in mechanical engineering in 1927, then owned another WWI Jenny, and a Standard J-1 which I rebuilt from a wreck. I sold it in 1929 and taught the young new owner to fly it from scratch. It is still in existence. Then I flew a New Standard D-25 for a few years, doing intense and successful barnstorming.

In 1931, I was the first person to purchase one of the revolutionary new Pitcairn autogiros, the PCA-2, with 330-hp engine. In it I did a lot of pioneer flying, including the first rotary-wing transcontinental flights and the first and only rotary-wing aerobatic exhibitions at major air meets all over the United States.

I went to work for United Air Lines in 1936 and flew the first modern airliner, the Boeing 247-D, until Kellett Autogiro Co. asked me to leave UAL to test-fly the first wingless aircraft to get approval. I flew close to 3,000 flights to and from the roof of the Philadelphia Post Office Building (1939-40). This was an experimental air mail contract with full success, the first scheduled rooftop operation in history.

During WWII, I flew for Eastern Air Lines at LaGuardia, and

I was also the chief test pilot for Columbia Aircraft, testing hundreds of Navy amphibians, while living nearby. Later, I moved back to my home in Poughkeepsie, New York, and drove 80 miles to LGA, then 92 miles to Idlewild (now JFK) for my airline trips.

The roads had heavy, wild traffic and I was driving 3,000 miles per month. I witnessed many crashes, sometimes barely avoiding being crashed into by fast drivers who frequently slid across the double line. I decided it would be safer to fly—even though it was at night over some very rugged mountains, water and populated areas.

So in 1952, I started commuting with a little BC12-D Taylorcraft with no radio, but IDL tower would give me light signals. In 1953, I bought a Stinson Voyager 108-1 and installed the first of the newly developed VORs. Then I could make the trips IFR, day and night. I was the only airline captain in the New York area who commuted by private airplane.

In 1956, I bought my first Bonanza, a C35, and installed a new and modern panel. That Bonanza served me for 37 years, during the rest of my tenure with EAL and later.

I also made numerous trips in it all over the US 48, Mexico and Canada.

While at EAL, I flew the twin engine DC-2 and DC-3, the four-engine DC-4, DC-7, four types of Constellations, the Lockheed L-188 Electra turboprop, and finally—for the last five years until retirement—the great four-jet DC-8. So I say I flew "Jennys to jets" and use that as my e-mail address: jennys2jets @juno.com.

In 1971, I bought a Baron 56TC, a real hotrod, and flew it many times to California and Florida and to Alaska. It was an exceptional airplane with big 380-hp Lycoming engines. I owned it for 30 years but sold it in 2001 and now fly my V35A. It is good, but I really do miss that high-performance 56TC.

While I had the C35, I taught and soloed my first grandson in it at age 16. He is now 45, a pure Bonanza pilot. I had previously taught and soloed my son in the Stinson, also at 16.

After retiring from EAL, I "un-retired" and bought a Bell 47 helicopter. I flew it under FAA Part 135 for several years and did a lot of police contract flying until the state of New York bought their own fleet

of Bell Jet Rangers. That put me out of business. I loved the helicopter flying, but it was hard work. I was on call all the time, and I did most of my own maintenance—continuous on a helicopter.

I am instrument current and have ATP-5945, A&P-2906, Naval Aviator-4821, each only four digits. I was a USMCR-commissioned pilot, beginning in 1930.

I have spent the equivalent of four solid years in the air (35,000 hours), not a record by any means. I still fly my V35A and I still own a lot of things with wheels: four cars, three motorcycles, one bicycle and two mower-tractors.

When I was 17, I taught myself the touch system of typing. I enjoy writing, so when I was invited to contribute some stories to the *ABS Magazine* about my experiences as a pilot, I accepted—and that soon led to my getting computer-literate.

This book is a collection of some of the stories published in the magazine over the last several years. I hope you enjoy them.

—*John M. Miller*
July, 2002

John Miller with his Model C Bonanza

Contents

John Miller and his "hotrod" 56TC Baron

1910: Glenn Curtiss

IN 1910 THERE WERE PROBABLY NO MORE THAN HALF A DOZEN FLYING MACHINES IN THE UNITED STATES CAPABLE OF CONTROLLED FLIGHT AND VERY, VERY FEW PEOPLE HAD EVER WITNESSED ONE OF THESE PRIMITIVE MACHINES ACTUALLY FLYING.

In fact, I am probably the only living person able to write firsthand about a flight Glenn Hammond Curtiss made on May 29, 1910, from Albany, New York, to New York City—152 miles over the Hudson River.

The *New York World* newspaper offered a prize of $10,000 for the first flight between New York City and Albany, the state capital, and I witnessed part of that flight when I was four and a half years old. The prize of 10,000 gold dollars was really generous and very tempting— probably about the equivalent of at least $200,000 in today's paper dollars. The flight did not have to be nonstop, for two stops were allowed, but it had to be made in one day between sunrise and sunset.

The Wright Brothers did not have a flying machine able to make such a flight so they had not entered. But Curtiss had built three or four flying machines in his Hammondsport Motorcycle factory and had advanced far ahead of the Wrights. With that prize money, he would be able to expand his flying machine production, so he built a machine especially for the attempt. This was to be one of the longest flights on record at that time—and entirely over water.

In addition to an extra large fuel tank, Curtiss attached two cylindrical floats under the lower wings of the biplane for emergency flotation if he were forced down in the river. He actually had made a test landing on the water of Keuka Lake at Hammondsport.

The machine had bamboo outriggers in the rear which supported a stabilizer surface and a rudder, and more bamboo outriggers in front to support an elevator. That arrangement made the aircraft rather unstable and difficult to fly, but it was the technology of the time—extremely flimsy by today's standards. Although it was very primitive, it was far ahead of the Wright Brothers Model B machine, which they had improved very little since 1908.

Curtiss would be entrusting his life to the engine that he and his employee, Mr. Kleckler, had designed and built in the motorcycle factory. In preparation for the risky attempt, Curtiss set up the plane in a tent on an island in the Hudson in the city limits of Albany and waited for fair weather.

A special steam railroad train was prepared to follow the plane down the river carrying reporters and dignitaries. Good weather was a long time coming and competing newspapers began accusing Curtiss of having cold feet. May 29 was a beautiful day, so Curtiss took off, the train following.

The newspapers in Pough-keepsie where I lived, halfway down the Hudson, had been giving daily reports on the delays so my father knew about the event. When May 29 dawned bright and sunny, he decided to go to the field south of Poughkeepsie which had been selected for a refueling stop to see if he could catch a glimpse of a real

Glenn Hammond Curtiss

PHOTOS COURTESY OF THE KANSAS AVIATION MUSEUM

Curtiss flying machine

flying machine for the first time. He took me with him.

As we left town on the electric trolley car, we heard several factory whistles blowing loudly. This led my dad to surmise that the flying machine must be already passing our city out over the river, but not visible to us. When we arrived at the field, however, it was on the ground. Curtiss was waiting for the man who was supposed to have brought the cans of gasoline for the refueling. Since he had not shown up, some men were draining gasoline out of the tank of

an automobile into an old-fashioned white ceramic pitcher and pouring it into the tank of the flying machine. I remember asking my dad why they were pouring water into the tank. It was the first time I had ever heard of gasoline, for my dad did not own an automobile until 1919.

We learned later that the "gasoline" man had already made the trip on several days and each time had been disappointed when the plane did not show up, so he was skeptical of the plan. Apparently, however, when he heard the factory

whistles blowing, he jumped on a streetcar just behind the one carrying my dad and me with two five-gallon cans of gasoline.

While the plane was on the ground, the special train had stopped. Its passengers had walked up the hill to the field, about a quarter mile. They were mostly men, but there were some women in their long dresses of the time. There were few others than local farm people in the crowd.

Remember, none of the people there had ever seen a flying machine. In fact, at that time, many people still claimed they were a fraud and some even considered them to be "Aginst God's will."

After the refueling was completed and the machine was ready to take off again, a man started the engine by pulling the wood propeller while inside the rear outriggers. Curtiss sat out in front of the engine, the fixed nose wheel just ahead of his feet.

The takeoff was very exciting, quick and short. The plane soared over some low trees and then turned south down the Hudson River at no more than 100 to 200 feet altitude. It soon disappeared in the distance, with the small crowd watching until it was no longer a speck.

I can still see that takeoff vividly in my mind, for Dad told me several times to be sure to remember it. He had done the same thing in

the previous month of April when he awakened me in my bed and carried me, wrapped up in a blanket, out of a window onto a flat roof to show me Halley's Comet—a beautiful stream of light across the sky!

The flight was successful and Curtiss won the Scientific American Trophy a third time, giving him permanent possession. The Wright Brothers had not competed for the trophy at all. I have a copy of the *Scientific American* for June 1910 that describes the flight in detail. The $10,000 prize money made it possible for Curtiss to expand his factory, which resulted in the great Curtiss Aeroplane and Motor Co. at Buffalo, New York—now only a memory.

The thrilling sight of that frail flying machine of bamboo, wire and cloth soaring up and off into the thin air has never left me. My dad's advice to try to remember it worked perfectly for me.

That flight changed my interest from steam locomotives to flying machines. From then on, I knew that I, too, would fly. While other boys had no objective in life, I knew precisely what I would do. The flying virus had infected me for life and I have had a wonderfully adventurous and rewarding flying career, since 1923.

18th Birthday: Solo!

ON MY 18TH BIRTHDAY, DECEMBER 15, 1923, I WAS PRACTICING "GRASS CUTTING"—THAT'S SKIMMING OVER THE GRASS IN A PLANE WITHOUT TAKING OFF— RIPPING UP AND DOWN THE FIELD, RISING A FEW INCHES ABOVE THE GRASS BEFORE SETTLING BACK AGAIN.

It was a beautiful day. My mind was filled with thoughts of what it would be like to be piloting the aircraft through turns and banks and bringing it home and landing it.

I was thinking it would be an appropriate thing to do on the 20th anniversary of the Wright Brothers' historic flight. I didn't really intend to go up at that particular moment, but the sharp, staccato sound of the engine suddenly split the silence like a fusillade of fire-crackers on the Fourth of July.

The Jenny whizzed toward a fence and I snapped back to reality. I knew if I got up in the air, I would be in deep trouble. I didn't know how to take a turn. I had read about it, that was all, but I was too close to the fence to stop so I had the choice of hitting it or bringing the plane up over it. I sure didn't want to hurt the fence—it wasn't my fence. I was faced with a now-or-never decision and I did for the first time what I would be doing thousands of times in the future: I pulled back the stick and roared into the air.

From then on, for at least an hour, I was in trouble. I was scared to death, but mostly I was concerned that I was going to hurt the airplane. I finally landed the plane in a better field, but I had to get it off again before the farmer got mad at me, so I took off right away and flew back to the original field.

As I taxied in, a farmer drove up in a pickup truck and asked me how much I would charge for a ride. He said he had a dollar and a half, so that was my asking price. I became a commercial pilot on my third solo!

When my passenger and I landed, two more customers were waiting. I made two more passenger hops at $5 each that day. I was really elated. You couldn't stop me. There were no regulations at all in those days, and I was free as a bird. Ⓜ

The farmer said he had a dollar and a half, so that was my asking price. I became a commercial pilot on my third solo!

John Miller with the Jenny he soloed in on his 18th birthday

PHOTO COURTESY OF JOHN MILLER

Free as a Bird: The 1920s

I T MAY BE HARD TO BELIEVE BUT THERE WAS A TIME, LESS THAN A LIFETIME AGO, WHEN THERE WERE NO FLYING REGULATIONS (OR EVEN DRIVER'S LICENSES) IN NEW YORK STATE. WHEN I STARTED FLYING IN LATE 1923, ONE OF ITS GREAT ATTRACTIONS WAS THE ABSOLUTE FREEDOM IN THE AIR. THERE WERE NO AVIATION REGULATIONS AT ALL.

John Miller with JN-4 Jenny powered by Curtiss OX-5 engine

I was as free as a bird. Up there aloft, one was completely alone—liberated. Without a radio, there was no way to communicate for help, so it was imperative to be self-reliant—or learn how to be. Flying was the "great adventure" of the time.

The airplanes were almost all WWI surplus types, mostly the Curtiss JN-4 or the Standard J-1 biplanes with two open cockpits. They had no electrical systems, no radios, no lights, no flaps, no airspeed indicators, no interphones. no engine starters, no heaters, no navigation systems, no fog-flying instruments and no wheel brakes—only a tailskid.

The shock absorbers were simple rubber bungee cords that produced great bounces if the landings were not good three-point. The altimeter had a single hand, which made a partial circle to 15,000 feet or so, entirely unattainable. We would set them to ground level. Flying was practically a continuous emergency!

There were no carburetor heaters, so dead-engine landings were routine when the carburetor iced and caused mysterious engine stoppages, resulting in exciting happy dead-stick landings or sad ones.

Carburetor icing was not yet understood. Curtiss had partly solved the problem on the OX-5 engines.

He reasoned that the trouble was simply failure of the gasoline to properly vaporize, so had installed permanent heaters that reduced the power. To get any real altitude, we had to disable them.

The air mail pilots finally did discover the carburetor ice solution, but most flying peasants knew nothing about carburetor ice. I was a member of the old National Air Pilots Association (NAPA), for air mail pilots, and read of the icing problems in the NAPA newsletters.

Navigation was done by a WWI magnetic compass and a pencil line on the map. The only maps available in the United States were the Rand-McNally state maps which showed railroads (no roads), towns and terrain such as mountains, rivers and lakes.

Maps sold for aviation were printed with red isogonal magnetic lines, known airfields (not airports in those days) and known elevations of peaks and various areas. I still have a mint condition Rand-McNally *Directory of Air Fields and Camp Grounds*, vintage 1923, which does not list a single airfield with a paved runway in the United States. There were none.

Brakeless, tailskid-type airplanes and paved runways were not at all compatible. The first paved runway I ever saw or landed on was in 1929 at Miami, built by PAA for Fokker three-engine airplanes which had tailwheels. It is now Miami International.

The first airplanes with nosewheels were the old Curtiss pre-WWI pusher airplanes. They were fixed, not steerable, and had a brake shoe that bore down on the tire, which was out in front of the pilot, who was out in front of everything else in the cold wind.

About 1932, Waco provided a new castering nosewheel on the Model N cabin biplane, but pilots were very suspicious of it. It was ahead of its time. The tailwheel and taildragger airplanes were directionally unstable on the ground, so they wanted to reverse direction very violently and destructively. It was called a ground loop. The taildragger airplane's only braking was provided by the friction of the tailskid on the sod. On a paved-surface runway, there was practically no effective braking.

Without brakes, the most effective directional control on ground roll was with the opposite aileron. The rudders were blanked by the fuselage in its tail-down position. They were ineffective unless a blast of power was used which, of course, increased the length of the roll.

Brakes came later, about 1928. Flying the real brakeless tailskid airplanes, the true taildraggers, is now a lost art. The modern type of steerable nosewheel is a great safety improvement, providing inherent directional stability on ground roll.

The interim types, with brakes and tailwheels, were suitable for paved runways. They included such larger airplanes as the DC-3 to the B-17, which had pilot-lockable tailwheels. The Lockheed Constellation and Douglas DC-4 airliners were the first large steerable nosewheel airplanes.

My fondest memories are of flying those old biplanes in the days before regulations. There was complete freedom of the air and we all took advantage of it. One sport I really enjoyed most on a fine summer day was to fly up into the scattered fluffy clouds and play around in them. It was both fun and valuable practice.

Instrument flying was started in 1926 by Howard Stark and was barely beginning to be practiced after the Lindbergh flight in 1927. By the time I was flying for a living in 1928, it was very rare for any airplane to be flown on instruments, except for the air mail pilots who had learned from Stark. So the clouds were sterile of airplanes.

In a Jenny, devoid of instruments, I could try to fly through the clouds without losing control. But if the time required to get out the other side was too long, I would get

My fondest memories are of flying those old biplanes in the days before regulations. There was complete freedom of the air and we all took advantage of it. I really enjoyed flying up into scattered fluffy clouds on a fine summer day and playing around in them. It was both fun and valuable practice.

into the classic spiral dive and plunge out of the bottom in a turn opposite of what I had sensed, just as Stark had described in his pamphlet.

It was exhilarating fun to plunge into the clouds, dive through the cloud valleys and canyons, circle the white peaks and castles, spin down through a cloud to break out of the bottom. The Jenny was perfectly docile in a spin and would spin as long as I could count, recovering in one turn. It was fun to loop up into the bottom of a cloud and come out of it on the back side of the loop.

All such flying was valuable practice in maneuvering, which became instinctive. Later, in the early military biplanes, I would practice inverted maneuvers and even flying through clouds inverted, with a turn indicator. Up there it was like bouncing around on a big soft mattress. When pulling out of a dive with one of those faster fighters, the wingtips made vortex trails of visible vapor. When the sun was directly behind, the little rainbow circles on the brilliant white clouds had the shadow of the airplane in their centers—a fine target for a simulated collision, ending inside the cloud.

With the later military fighters equipped with turn indicators, I would get valuable practice in some extremely turbulent clouds, good practice for later thunderstorm fly-

ing in my airline career. Aerobatic practice of that sort was valuable in developing instinctive flying. The airplane would answer my thoughts, without me thinking about which way to move the controls.

I taught myself proficient instrument flying with the guidance of Stark's pamphlets. My engineering training was of great help in understanding the reasons for everything involved. It paid off, for when I took my flight check for an ATP, I was limited to the turn-and-bank indicator (Eastern Air Lines' old test).

In the early 1920s, it was seriously proposed to have the Army regulate all flying. The flying community, such as it then existed, squashed the idea. So a long period without regulations continued until the Air Commerce Act of 1926 went into effect in 1927, with licensing and flying regulations becoming mandatory in 1928. Barnstorming became difficult under the new regulations and soon ended.

The period from 1919 to 1929 was the barnstorming era with WWI surplus aircraft mostly, but with some new production aircraft from 1926 to 1930. The surplus aircraft were open biplanes, mostly two-seat trainers, unfit for carrying passengers cross-country in commercial operations due to their short range and low speed, low load and low safety. Also,

the war surplus or pre-war designed surplus engines did not have a long life or the best of reliability. So flying in that period was limited mainly to flight instruction, sport flying, local passenger hopping and itinerant barnstorming.

The latter was my forte and very successful, but with a new production, excellent airplane designed specifically for barnstorming—the new Standard D-25, five-place open biplane with the latest engine, the Wright J-5, 225 hp. This was the same type used by Lindbergh on his famous transatlantic flight.

This plane temporarily stimulated barnstorming and 1927 was the busiest barnstorming period. That was also the most lucrative year for the famous Gates Flying Circus. At the end of the season, the new regulations and inspection system grounded all of their war surplus planes and put the Gates Circus out of business. It had safely carried at least a quarter of a million passengers, probably more, on short hops.

I worked as a mechanic for the circus in the summer of 1927, then I got a plane of my own, a Hispano-Suiza-powered Standard J-1, the same as those in the circus. I carefully overhauled the airplane and had no trouble getting it licensed. I sold it in 1929 and taught the new owner to fly it. He flew it for several years

and it is still in existence, being restored.

During the period of 1925 to about 1929, a number of three-place open biplanes with open cockpits were designed and on the market. They were powered by the ancient pre-war designed Curtiss OX-5 engine, which was built in large quantities during WWI and used mainly in the JN-4 Jenny. There was a great surplus of those engines so they were used in the newly designed biplanes of various makes, such as the Waco, Swallow, Eaglerock, American Eagle, Travel Air 2000 and others.

Waco

Swallow

Walter Beech and Lloyd Stearman were associated in the production of the Travel Air 2000. The eight-cylinder, 90-hp water-

Travel Air 2000

cooled V-8 OX-5 engines had exposed valve rocker arms which were not even covered by cowling. They were lubricated between flights by sticking the spout of an ordinary squirt-type oil can into the little oil holes in the rocker arms. Thus, a lot of surplus oil would blow back into the faces of the pilot and passengers in the open cockpits. If you ever wondered why the old-time pilots often wore those white scarves, they were to wipe oil from their faces and goggles.

The original OX-5, 90-hp engines had a single magneto. The later ones, the OXX-6, rated at 110 hp, had dual magnetos, and there were fewer of those. When the single magneto failed, which was often, a dead engine landing was made in a hurry—either a rather happy occurrence or a disaster. Beginning in about 1926, some new engine designs such as the Warner and Kinner began to appear to go into those same biplanes and later into the cabin types.

That era of open-cockpit biplanes, powered by the 90-hp OX-5 engines, engendered a new airshow sport—the popular OX-5

races. The engines had to be unmodified and the only changes allowed in the aircraft itself were a cover for the front cockpit to reduce drag and removal of the front windshield.

The pilots flew the races with a light load of fuel and no passenger. I even saw some take out the front seat cushions to reduce weight! However, I knew that when the airplanes were flown at high speed, the wings were at a very low angle of attack, thereby flying at low lift-to-drag ratio (L/D) with high drag.

I won a few of those races by secretly loading heavy sandbags in the covered front cockpit of a Travel Air 2000 and flight testing to get the right load for maximum speed. The wings then flew at a higher L/D angle of attack and the fuselage was pointed better into the airstream. It took longer to take off, but I later gained on my competition and won.

I was challenged as having "souped up" the engine, but the losers never did find out about the heavy sandbags. They didn't know much about aerodynamics, if anything. I could have used a passenger for weight, but then the cockpit would be open and create unwanted drag. I had a snap-on cover for the cockpit.

As I remember, the first production cabin airplane was the Stinson cabin biplane with the early Wright

J-4 radial engine of 200 hp. It was of typical welded steel tube fuselage and wood wing structure, fabric covered. One of those was used by Howard Stark to fly the mail, and in which he developed the method of using the turn-and-bank indicator to recover from the fatal spiral dives and to safely fly in fog.

Fairchild produced a very successful cabin monoplane with radial engine, and Robinson, in St. Louis, put a three-place cabin monoplane with an OX-5 engine on the market, called the Robin. It was later acquired by Curtiss-Wright and they installed a 165-hp Wright radial engine. That was the plane used by "Wrong Way" Corrigan for his remarkable flight to Ireland. Those were some of the first U.S. cabin

Curtiss "Robin" Model C

airplanes built in any quantity.

Lockheed developed their outstanding all-wood Vega and the Orion, which were used for record 'round-the-world and transatlantic flights. Lindbergh used the Orion for many long-distance exploration

flights. Bellanca built a fine cabin airplane which was flown nonstop to Germany by Clarence Chamberlin, and Clyde Pangborn flew one in the first nonstop flight across the Pacific—Japan to Wenatchee, Washington.

Actually, the Europeans were far ahead of the United States in producing cabin airplanes, but in very low numbers. This was the era of the steel-tube fuselage, wood wing spars and fabric covering. The first monoplanes began to appear with the same type structures, such as the six-place Stinson Detroiter and the Travel Air 6000 with Wright radial engines, which were replaced by the metal

Stinson "Detroiter"

aircraft of today.

Just as in World War I, great advances in aircraft design resulted from World War II. In fact, Bonanzas and Barons are direct descendants of airplane design technology learned by the engineers at Beech Aircraft Co. The design of the Bonanza started before the war ended.

We should not forget that Harry Reiter, a Beech test pilot, was killed during the development of the Bonanza. Ⓜ

1927-28: Rules and Regulations

New Department of Commerce rules and regulations for licensing of pilots and inspection of airplanes were being set up in 1927 and were to become mandatory in 1928. Many World War I surplus airplanes were in bad condition and were being rejected and grounded by the new inspectors.

Since there was no office on the field, the inspector gave me the exams—which took most of the day—in his government car. He would read a topic from a manual and then ask me to write down how I would solve the problem or perform the work.

I decided I could probably qualify for one of the new mechanics licenses due to my previous experience, therefore, I wrote to Washington, D.C., and asked for an application form. I soon received word that an inspector had been assigned for the new licensing at Roosevelt Field on Long Island and that he would be driving the 80 or so miles to the little grass field at Poughkeepsie to give me the necessary exams required for the mechanics license.

It was explained to me that the newly licensed war surplus airplanes had to be serviced by licensed mechanics who were in very short supply. For that reason, it was neces-sary to get mechanics licensed as soon as possible. They were having diffi-culty finding men who could pass the examination. The ex-military mechanics had by that time already secured jobs in other occupations and had families.

Since there was no hangar or office on the field, the inspector gave me the exams—which took most of the day—in his government car. He would read a topic from a manual and then ask me to write down how I would solve the problem or perform the work. The morning was spent either writing my answers a paragraph at a time or verbally answering questions.

The types of airplanes in com-mon use at the time were the war surplus Curtiss JN-4 and the Standard J-1—very similar WWI training airplanes. The questions were about repairing the woodwork and the metal fittings, making up and splicing control and structural cables, and rigging and inspecting all the struc-tures, controls, shock absorbers, etc.

There were also questions about how to re-cover the wings and control surfaces with fabric by proper rib-stitching, taping, doping, etc. I had done all of that and had thor-oughly studied the subjects in books.

The afternoon was spent on the subject of engines and propellers. The ones in use in civil aviation were mainly the old Curtiss OX-5 types, the Hispano-Suiza and the Liberty. I had studied the engine manual on each engine so I passed the test easily, even though I had only actually worked on the OX-5.

The inspector seemed rather impressed, gave me a full score and issued my A&P license #2906 that I have used ever since. Ⓜ

Howard Stark: The 1-2-3 System

HOWARD STARK WAS BORN BEFORE THE TURN OF THE 20TH CENTURY ON A FARM AT PAWLING, NEW YORK. THIS TYPICAL FARM BOY WAS DRAFTED INTO THE U.S. ARMY IN WORLD WAR I, AND SINCE HE KNEW HOW TO DRIVE AN AUTOMOBILE, NOT A COMMON SKILL AT THAT TIME, HE WAS ASSIGNED AS THE DRIVER FOR A GENERAL.

While in France, he observed the military airplanes and decided he would like to fly. But without the required education, he was not accepted for transfer to flight training. Eddie Rickenbacker, a driver for General Pershing, had been accepted without the required education because of his fame as an automobile race driver. Rickenbacker became the ranking "ace" of American pilots in France. (I had the honor of knowing Capt. Eddie well and worked for him as a captain on Eastern Air Lines.)

After World War I was over, many Jenny training planes were sold as surplus to Curtiss, their original manufacturer, in Mineola, New York. Curtiss advertised them for sale for only $500, about one-twentieth of their original price, together with some instruction for flying them. In the early 1920s, $500 was the equivalent of perhaps $10,000 in today's market—quite an accomplishment for a country farm worker.

Howard saved the $500 purchase price while working on his father's farm and driving a car for a nearby family. He bought one of those surplus Jennys, and was assisted in assembling it at Curtiss Field at the factory, then was given a mere two hours of flying instruction. That's about eight hours less than is usually required for learning to fly a safe solo.

There were no aviation regulations in those days and Howard flew the airplane to his father's farm, crossing Long Island Sound on the way—a really surprising navigational accomplishment for such a neophyte pilot. Unfortunately, his inexperience showed when he crashed while attempting to land in a very short field.

The way to make a living with your airplane in those early days was to barnstorm from place to place, taking passengers up on their first air flights. There were no airlines, and only the Post Office Airmail Service to California. In 1926, the Post Office contracted with private corporations to take over the air mail flights. By that time Howard owned a very modern airplane for its day—a Stinson cabin biplane, one of the first enclosed-cabin airplanes manufactured in the United States.

Colonial Airways, the New York to Boston air mail contractor, had a shortage of modern airplanes and tried to buy the Stinson cabin biplane from Howard. Because he wouldn't sell it, they finally rented it and hired him to fly it. That's how Howard started to fly the mail between New York (Hadley Field, New Brunswick, New Jersey) and Boston.

There was no known way to fly through the fog, so all flying in bad weather was made down low, under the clouds. Attempts to fly higher into the clouds was very dangerous. Flying under the overcast also caused a lot of collisions with terrain or other obstructions. So flying the mail was a risky occupation. There were many fatalities, which gave aviation a bad reputation that was much worse than it deserved.

The Sperry Gyroscope Company attempted to solve the problem of flying in the fog. They invented a small gyroscopic instrument called a Turn Indicator and delivered samples to the Army Air Service. Two experienced Army pilots, Capt. Ocker and Lt. Crane, were assigned the task of evaluating the instrument. They worked on the problem for about a year at San Antonio, Texas.

Their report, published as a book, concluded that it was not possible to fly continuously by referring to the instrument in the fog without losing control of the airplane. In fact, the report said that one could not fly for more than about three minutes before losing control.

In the meantime, most of the air mail planes had been equipped with turn indicators, but the pilots soon discovered the same problem as Ocker and Crane. They could use it occasionally to zoom up through a layer of clouds to get up in the clear air to pass over the mountains by keeping the airplane going straight. But their attempts to fly for more

Except for the fact that he had been told what it was for, the turn indicator was a mystery to Howard. He noticed, however, when he kept his hands off the controls and simply kept the airplane in a straight heading by referring to the turn indicator and the compass—using his feet on the rudder controls to do so—that his airplane flew itself very well.

than three minutes or so always resulted in loss of control—and quite often ended in disaster when they suffered severe vertigo and disorientation resulting in a false sense of turning and diving.

Stinson's cabin biplane was equipped with a turn indicator but, fortunately for Howard, he had not heard of the Ocker and Crane experiments and did not know of their conclusion that it was impossible to fly with the turn indicator in the fog for longer than a few minutes. Except for the fact that he had been told what it was for, the turn indicator was a mystery to him. He noticed, however, when he kept his hands off the controls and simply kept the airplane in a straight heading by referring to the turn indicator and the compass—using his feet on the rudder controls to do so—that his airplane flew itself very well. The Stinson cabin biplane had a reputation as a very stable airplane.

Howard found that he could fly the entire distance between New York and Boston that way. He simply adjusted the stabilizer trim to maintain his desired altitude, all without touching the control stick.

Across the route of the New York-Boston air mail line there is a low mountain ridge in the vicinity of the Connecticut River. When the cloud ceiling was lower than that ridge, it was sometimes not possible for the pilots to get past the ridge, even by an end-run around the south end at the shore of Long Island Sound where the fog would usually be right down to the surface. When this situation occurred and the pilots could not find a slight gap to squeeze through, they would either have to land and wait for conditions to improve or return to their starting point. This problem caused some fatal accidents when the pilots tried to get over the ridge in the fog.

In this modern day of aviation, people do not realize how many pilots lost their lives flying the mail as well as others flying in bad weather during those pioneer days. As a matter of fact, from 1918 to 1926 during the Post Office operation of the Transcontinental Airmail Service alone, there were 42 fatalities.

Even in fair weather, much of the flying was done at low altitude so the pilots could become very familiar with the terrain and the obstructions along their routes. In bad weather, some flying was commonly done under ceilings as low as 100 feet, or even lower. Of course, there were accidents and that was the very reason Colonial Airways had a shortage of airplanes, and the reason they needed Howard's airplane.

Howard discovered that when he flew at a low altitude with his hands off the control stick, as I have just described, that he could adjust the longitudinal trim to climb over the ridge. When he was past it, he would readjust the trim to descend to the original low altitude again on the other side. He recorded the time required to safely pass over the ridge and concluded after several such flights that if he could do it in *fair* weather, then he should also be able to do it in *foggy* weather.

He did exactly that when the cloud ceiling was very low, arriving at Boston with the mail while the westbound pilot had found it necessary to return to Boston, unable to get over the ridge. Howard would then take that pilot's mail back to New York successfully, much to the embarrassment of the other pilots. They were very rankled when this country farmer pilot outflew them.

When he explained to the other pilots—all of them experienced ex-Army pilots from WWI—how he had done it, they refused to believe him. They thought he had used a secret gap he had discovered in the ridge. After one more pilot lost his life, they were finally convinced.

This type of flying was only done in a practically straight line. Whenever Howard attempted to fly in a higher overcast for practice in making turns, he would quickly lose control due to severe vertigo and disorientation. Such attempts invariably resulted in a spiral dive out of the base of the overcast. That was what had happened to several other pilots who had experienced fatal accidents when they dove into the ground or their airplanes disintegrated in the air due to the high-speed spiral dives.

As I said, Howard had not read the Ocker and Crane report and literature about other pilots having this same difficulty. So he assumed that since such an instrument existed, *someone* must know or had known how to use it. So he set out to teach himself how.

The fact was that even the pilots for Sperry, the originator, and Pioneer Instrument Co., the manufacturer, were unable to use the turn indicator successfully. All of them lost control. So flying by means of the turn indicator was considered to be just an unproven theory.

It was assumed that instrument flying would not be possible until an entirely different type of instrument was developed. Later, of course, Sperry did develop the gyroscopic artificial horizon and the directional gyro. All three instruments in various forms are used to this day and are the backbone of instrument flying.

Without the false information about the turn indicator, my friend Howard was able to analyze the reason for always getting into a spiral dive when he attempted to fly turns in the bottom of the overcast clouds. The false sensations had to be forcibly ignored by the pilot. Then the turn had to be stopped—first with the rudder, then the wings leveled by means of the gravity ball indicator. Finally, the airspeed had to be adjusted with the elevator controls.

Howard accomplished what the scientists at Sperry and all of the other pilots had failed to do: He found that, first of all, the pilot had to learn to ignore the false sensations that were caused by vertigo and must believe the instruments only.

Second, to recover lost control when the airplane would start a spiral dive, the turn had to be stopped first by reference to the turn needle by pressure on the rudder pedals. Then the ball had to be centered by the ailerons to level the wings. Third, the dive had to be stopped by means of the elevators and the airspeed indicator and only in that same order. And Howard knew the reasons for it.

He called it the Stark 1-2-3 System. It consisted of scanning the instruments and making corrections for each reading. In only that way was it possible to regain and maintain control when one got into what otherwise was almost certainly a fatal spiral dive.

This was Stark's important discovery and it is still known to this day as the Stark 1-2-3 System. It must be learned by all pilots when they obtain their instrument ratings.

With the assistance of his wife, Howard wrote and published a pamphlet called "Blind or Instrument Flying?" By "blind flying," he meant "trying to fly in fog without instruments," hence the use of the question mark. He distributed the pamphlet by mail, and many pilots bought it. He did not realize that he should have submitted the information to a scientific publication. He gave me one and I used it successfully.

After instructing the Colonial Airways pilots in the use of his 1-2-3 System, word spread about Howard. When the information reached National Air Transport, the contractor air mail line from New York to Chicago, they requested that Howard teach their chief pilots to use the turn indicator properly. Boeing Air Transport, the air mail contractor from Chicago to the west coast, also used Howard's instruction. (Those two airlines later combined and, along with Varney Airlines, formed today's United Air Lines.)

The word spread quickly and American Airlines, Transcontinental Air Transport and Western Air Express followed. The latter two later combined to form today's TWA.

The Royal Dutch Airlines (KLM) hired Howard to go to Holland to teach their pilots. Pilots of Lufthansa and British Imperial Airways (now British Airways) were soon using Howard's 1-2-3 System, too. He became a pilot for Eastern Air Transport (later EAL) and taught their pilots.

He wrote some more updated pamphlets on the subject of instrument flying as the artificial horizon

---

The Royal Dutch Airlines (KLM) hired Howard to go to Holland to teach their pilots. Pilots of Lufthansa and British Imperial Airways (now British Airways) were soon using Howard's 1-2-3 System, too.

In 1929, the well-known Jimmy Doolittle was able to make complete flights under the hood from takeoff to landing and did so before many witnesses, resulting in a great amount of publicity. Soon he was called the "Father of Instrument Flying." Of course, his accomplishment was very important and outstanding, but was he really the actual "father" of instrument flying when Howard Stark was the first to fly in actual fog in 1926?

and directional gyro were developed and the radio range navigation system was installed.

Howard became very well known in airline aviation. The U.S. Department of Commerce, Aeronautics Branch, employed him to teach their inspectors to use the turn indicator so they could make regulations for instrument (IFR) flying and finally for air traffic control, as we know it today.

By 1929, Sperry had developed the gyroscopic artificial horizon and the directional gyro, both standard equipment in one form or another in all today's well-equipped airplanes. In that year, the well-known James Doolittle practiced using all three instruments, plus a radio direction finder in a small Army training plane, under the hood and with a safety pilot, at Mitchell Field, Long Island.

Jimmy Doolittle was able to make complete flights under the hood from takeoff to landing and did so before many witnesses, resulting in a great amount of publicity about his demonstrations. Soon he was called the "Father of Instrument Flying." Of course, his accomplishment was very important and outstanding, but was he really the actual "father" of instrument flying when Howard Stark was the first to fly in actual fog in 1926?

In January 1936 Howard was flying a Stinson Model S, a four-place cabin airplane for the Department of Commerce, with orders to fly to the West Coast to give more instruction to D.O.C. inspectors. At Cheyenne, Wyoming, on January 16, after a few days delay due to severe winter weather, he got good weather reports and started to fly across that high route to Salt Lake City. He had never been there before and the plane and equipment were barely able to make the necessary altitude and distance by visual flying only.

He ran into a severe unforecast snowstorm and made an emergency landing in very deep snow in a remote area of the Wasatch Mountains. He froze to death trying to walk out in deep snow and minus 20 degree temperature.

The Stinson had nosed over onto its back in deep snow, undamaged and was quickly covered by new snow so that it was not visible to air searchers. It was found by a sheep herder the next spring. Howard's body was not found until four years later. And so ended the career of a remarkable man, sadly, too early.

Howard Stark was so shy, so self-effacing and modest, that he never retained a public relations firm. Of course, the Army Air Service extracted all the publicity possible out of Doolittle's accomplishment—and he deserved it. But in my opinion, Howard Stark is really the almost-forgotten but true father of today's instrument flying. His discovery saved many lives. It is a basic ingredient of today's airline, military and general aviation.

I am very thankful that I knew Howard so well. I feel he is an unsung heroic pioneer of aviation.

May 1927: Watching Lindy

IN MAY 1927, A NUMBER OF PILOTS WERE MAKING PREPARATIONS AT ROOSEVELT FIELD AND CURTISS FIELD ON LONG ISLAND TO COMPETE FOR THE ORTEIG PRIZE OF $25,000 FOR THE FIRST NONSTOP FLIGHT BETWEEN NEW YORK AND PARIS. I FREQUENTLY WENT OUT TO MINEOLA, LONG ISLAND, TO WATCH THE PREPARATIONS.

I was a mechanical engineering student at the Pratt Institute of Technology in Brooklyn, New York, sometimes cutting my classes to watch the pilots. I had done some flying before that, starting in 1923 while in my fourth year of high school.

One day, I was standing beside my friend Howard Stark watching Charles Lindbergh and his plane. Howard was the first person to successfully fly on instruments in the fog using the new turn indicator. He had discovered the proper way to use the instrument and had published an instruction pamphlet that he sold by mail called the Stark 1-2-3 System. It is still used today.

Lindbergh, an air mail pilot who had flown a newly built monoplane across the continent with the intention of flying to Paris, France, was working around his airplane. While we were standing there, someone pointed out Howard to Lindbergh, who walked over to speak to him. He complimented Howard on the pamphlet, a copy of which he had purchased by mail.

Lindbergh had taught himself to fly in the fog using Howard's method. Although Howard had mentioned to me that he had sold the pamphlet to Lindbergh, he was a very shy person and had not introduced himself to Lindbergh. I did not join in the conversation for I was a very junior member of the aviation scene at the time.

We both had looked into the cockpit of the Ryan airplane and saw the turn indicator on the panel. In addition, there was a Pioneer earth inductor compass, operated by a little anemometer on the top of the fuselage. Those two instruments were on the cutting edge of technology at the time and certainly helped make the famous flight possible. As far as I know, all of the other airplanes in preparation for the flight had turn indicators, but Howard and I doubted whether all the other pilots were really proficient in their use.

I was at the field again on the day before Lindbergh took off and heard rumors that he was planning to leave the next morning. I stayed up all night, most of the time in the lobby of the Garden City Hotel, waiting for the event.

As I watched Lindbergh take off on that cloudy morning, I really worried about the plane clearing the wires and the trees. After he was out of sight in the murk, I said to myself and to others nearby that we would probably never see that poor guy again. I thought he would probably disappear like Old Glory—the Fokker Universal monoplane I had watched in its preparations but had missed its takeoff—and the big Sikorsky biplane that had crashed and burned while attempting to take off with a too-heavy load of fuel.

But Lindbergh made it back and later, when the big welcoming parade was held in New York City on 5th Avenue, I watched it from a ninth floor windowsill at the office of my

As I watched Lindbergh take off on that cloudy morning, I really worried about the plane clearing the wires and the trees. After he was out of sight in the murk, I said to myself and to others nearby that we would probably never see that poor guy again.

aunt who ran a little employment agency for office girls. It was a perfect grandstand seat for that huge parade.

In 1930, the Lindberghs kept their Lockheed Sirius in the Bendix hangar at Teterboro. At that time I was flying professionally at Teterboro Airport, and I used to help him push it in and out of the hangar when they went on various flights. I did not really get acquainted with Lindbergh because I did not wish to be another pushy person; there were plenty of those already. However, he voluntarily gave me an 8x10 autographed photo of himself which I still have— and highly prize.

Many years later on March 23, 1992, I was in Washington, D.C., visiting the National Air & Space Museum. The *Spirit of St. Louis* Ryan NX211 had been taken down from its usual place hanging from the ceiling and was being cleaned. Care was being taken to avoid wiping off the honorable exhaust stains.

The engine cowling was removed and I could again look into the cockpit, but only from about a 15-foot distance this time because of barriers. It reminded me of the last time I had looked into that cockpit 65 years before.

I wonder how many pilots today would be able to fly with just a turn indicator, magnetic compass, earth inductor compass, airspeed indicator and altimeter—having no forward visibility and no radio navigation avionic system—and keep awake for 33 and a half hours! Ⓜ

Lindbergh's Lockheed Sirius (circa 1930)

My Flying Circus Job

A SHORT TIME AFTER I GOT MY MECHANIC'S LICENSE, THE FAMOUS GATES FLYING CIRCUS CAME TO TOWN TO HOP PASSENGERS ON THAT SAME LITTLE FIELD IN POUGHKEEPSIE, KNOWN THEN AS POUGHKEEPSIE AIRPORT, NOW LONG GONE. AT THAT TIME THE CIRCUS WAS FLYING FOUR J-1 STANDARDS AND ONE LARGER PLANE, A WWI CURTISS R-4 THAT HAD A BIG, NOISY, POWERFUL 400-HP LIBERTY ENGINE.

I introduced myself to the pilot of the Curtiss and told him I was a licensed A&P mechanic. He seemed very surprised to find a licensed mechanic in an area where there was only one old, still unlicensed surplus Jenny.

When they had finished flying on a very busy Sunday, he told me there were two severely blowing exhaust valves on the engine and asked if I could repair them. Of course, I said I could—although I had never before been within shouting distance of a big Liberty engine. But I had studied the manual carefully.

When I confirmed that I could have it ready by the next Saturday, he hired me to do the work. I worked hard at it during the week, removing the overhead camshaft and hand-grinding the two valves, which fortunately were on the same side.

When the pilot returned the next Saturday, he was so pleased that he offered me a job with the circus to act as crew chief on that airplane, which I accepted. He was in a hurry to fly to Pittsfield, Massachusetts, where the circus was to operate that weekend. So I left my motorcycle there on the field, got into the airplane without even my toothbrush and rode up to Pittsfield.

We were greeted by an enthusiastic crowd, and they became even more so when they heard that big engine roar to take off and make steep climbing turns with four passengers aboard. The circus stayed very busy until dark when we finally went to a hotel and I was able to call my parents to tell them where I was and what I was doing. I also asked them to please have my brother retrieve my motorcycle at Poughkeepsie airport.

The next day, Sunday, business was so brisk that it became the biggest revenue day and weekend in the history of the circus, obviously due to the great publicity of the Lindbergh flight the previous May (which I had cut classes to witness).

Pilots were all making rapid and spectacular short hops with full loads of four passengers at $2.50 each. They took off one right behind the other and flew in a tight circle around the field.

Toward the end of the day when I was watching the R-4 make its unusually steep climbing turn, the engine suddenly quit and smoke, oil and small fragments of something trailed behind the curved path of the plane. The very skilled and colorful pilot, Ive McKinney, easily landed back on the field and rolled to a stop right on the line in front of the crowd, just as if it were a normal flight.

Of course, I was alarmed because I thought I might have made some mistake in my work on the engine. It turned out, however, that it was a piston rod that had failed and wrecked

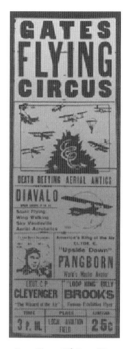

The touring Gates Flying Circus owned by Ivan Gates was by 1927 drawing as many as 30,000 spectators to each performance and selling rides to 100,000 passengers a year. Its permanent headquarters were near Teterboro Airport in New Jersey.

Ive McKinney in a Curtiss R-4 with a 400-hp Liberty engine

the engine. Ive asked me to stay in Pittsfield with a helper to change the engine with a replacement that would be shipped up from Lodi, New Jersey, near Teterboro Airport.

By the time Ive returned the next Friday, we had successfully completed the work and were ready to fly west to Troy, New York, for the weekend circus operation at an airstrip owned by the Ford Motor Co. at Green Island. This flight turned out to be a rather scary one, and that is one reason I am telling this story.

Troy was some 25 nm northwest of Pittsfield. There were hills in between and a low ceiling that day of no more than 800 feet at Pittsfield. Since no weather reports were available for Albany or Troy in those days, there was an obvious problem—but that didn't bother Ive.

With only an ordinary road map—no sectionals in 1927—he took off and headed northwest. Through a few thin spots in the overcast, we could see it was probably not more than 2,000 feet thick.

We could see the higher ground ahead was obscured by the cloud cover. No instrument flying was being done at that time, for Howard Stark had started it only the year before, and only a few of the air mail pilots were learning to fly by the lone turn indicators in the mail planes. They used Stark's mail-order pamphlets to instruct themselves, and they were able to zoom up through the stratus layers over the Allegheny mountains with the turn indicators, developing the skill

for continuous flying in the murk.

Ive McKinney knew absolutely nothing about instrument flying, but he had experience with briefly zooming up through stratus layers without any outside vision.

With his girlfriend, my helper and me in the front cockpit, he opened the engine wide. After getting full speed with the biplane, perhaps 115 mph, right under the base of the overcast he zoomed upward into the ceiling.

The airplane staggered and fell

How Ive found that little airstrip at Troy in that darkness, I don't know. As he circled it, we could just barely see the line of four Standards tied down, and he made a beautiful landing with no lights on either the airplane or the airstrip. Ive surely didn't have any night vision problem.

off on one wing and dived back out of the bottom of the clouds, with the ground right in front of the nose of the airplane. Ive recovered and repeated the same procedure with the same results. On the third try, however, just as the plane was beginning to run out of speed, we could see a spot of the setting sun.

With the airplane staggering and Ive watching the sun to help hold the right angle of climb and one direction toward it, he was able to stagger out of the clouds up on top.

Of course, during all of this hazardous performance, I was just about scared to death, for I was enough of a pilot to know the danger and was aware of the long record of many accidents when pilots got into the clouds during that era (and even today).

When we were finally up and over the clouds, in the clear and the red sun just about to set, it was so beautiful up there—my first time! But the clouds ranged far ahead. How were we to know when we were over Troy? Finally a hole in the clouds appeared, but down at ground level the sun had set and it was very dark down there!

That didn't disturb Ive. The sun was long gone. He made a beautiful helical descent with 45-degree banks right down through that little hole. We found ourselves flying in darkness, but fortunately the lights of Albany and Troy were visible.

How Ive found that little airstrip at Troy in that darkness, I don't know. As he circled it, we could just barely see the line of four Standards tied down, and he made a beautiful landing in the dark. No lights on either the airplane or the airstrip. Ive surely didn't have any night vision problem.

No one was there—all the pilots had gone to the hotel. We got a ride and joined them happily. After dinner, I went to bed, and drifted off to sleep with wonderful, scary memories.

The chief pilot of the circus was Clyde Pangborn, who later became a very good friend of mine along with Ive and the other pilots—Lee Mason, Joe James and Roy Ahearn. Pang later made the first trans-Pacific nonstop flight from Japan to Washington State in 1931, plus other notable flying. The skilled parachute jumper/wingwalker was "Duke" Krantz, called Diavalo on the circus posters. All are gone to the forever now.

The Gates Flying Circus ended shortly after the "play" at Troy when the Department of Commerce inspector grounded all of their old war surplus airplanes. I went off to go flying by myself.

Although the Ivan R. Gates Flying Circus is no more, I treasure my memories and the privilege of having been a small part of it. Ⓜ

1928: The Poppy Drop

I N 1928 I WAS FLYING A PAIR OF WORLD WAR I AIRPLANES AT THE OLD POUGHKEEPSIE (NEW YORK) AIRPORT, LATER REPLACED BY THE PRESENT DUCHESS COUNTY AIRPORT, WHERE I STILL FLY. THE TWO AIRPLANES WERE A JN-4 JENNY AND A J-1 STANDARD. THE LATTER WAS POWERED BY A 220-HP HISPANO-SUIZA WATER-COOLED, V-8 ENGINE FROM A SPAD, WHICH WAS A GOOD ENGINE FOR ITS DAY.

PHOTO COURTESY OF JOHN MILLER

John with rebuilt/remodeled J-1 biplane, before its test flight on May 6, 1928.

On May 29 that year, the day before Memorial Day, a group of American Legion men came to the grass field at the hangarless airport and asked a favor of me. The men told me a bronze plaque was to be dedicated in memory of Poughkeepsie men who had lost their lives in the World War in 1917-1918.

The ceremony was to be held on Memorial Day, instead of as originally planned for the November 11 Armistice Day, which would have been the 10th anniversary of the signing of the armistice ending the war. The plaque had already been installed on the old City Hall on Main Street, but had been covered by a shroud that was to be dropped during this planned ceremony sponsored by the Legion.

They asked me to participate in the dedication by dropping from the air over the assemblage a large number of the little artificial poppies sold by Legionnaires all over the United States to raise funds ("Poppies from Flanders Fields"). I was happy to do so. The men said that a very large crowd was expected to assemble in front of City Hall for the ceremony, including one or two army generals, many veterans and their relatives—and politicians, of course.

Several buglers would be standing in front of the plaque to play *Taps* just before the shroud was dropped to expose it to view. The timing of dropping of the poppies was to be very precise.

As you who are old enough to remember, the European War (later named WWI) armistice was signed, according to legend, at the 11th minute of the 11th hour of the 11th day of the 11th month of 1918. Therefore, it was planned to have the buglers sound *Taps* so as to finish just as the poppies started falling. That required precise timing. I agreed to try to comply, and since one of the men who worked for the railroad had an accurate Hamilton watch, I synchronized my Waltham wristwatch with it. They then left a large box of the poppies.

The straight-line distance from the field to the target was 4.5 miles, which would take just that number of minutes at the 65-70 mph cruising speed of the biplane against an expected 5 mph headwind. However, I planned to take off early and pass over the target exactly on time.

Main Street and the course to the target were almost parallel and converging. The street was level to the target, but then dropped downhill for a little more than half a mile to the half-mile-wide Hudson River. The Main Street trolley car tracks, with their overhead 600-volt wires, also led right down to the dock at the river. (Remember that.) There was a big iron railroad bridge about three-eighths of a mile to the north of that point.

My plan was to charge along Main Street, descending toward the target in a silent, power-off glide so as to get an accurately timed drop directly over the crowd at low altitude without engine noise that would drown out the sound of *Taps*. Of course, that would be bending the new air regulations not a little. It was to be a complete surprise event. After making the drop, I planned to continue the silent glide down the grade of Main Street for about a block or two, then add power gradually and fly away over the river. That afternoon, I made a practice flight at higher altitude to test the timing.

Memorial Day turned out to be perfect weather, clear and cool with a slight northwest breeze. I had the plane out and ready for warm-up and was expecting another pilot friend to sit in the cockpit while I cranked the big 9-foot, 2-inch left-hand Hamilton wood propeller myself. (I still have it.) I was 6 foot-2.5 inches tall, and weighed 175 pounds. I didn't allow anyone else to crank the prop for it was not only bigger than most propellers, but left-hand propellers were uncommon and decidedly unsafe for an inexperienced person.

A nonpilot friend was ready to ride in the front cockpit to dump the poppies overboard on my signal. The big water-cooled engine required ample time to warm up. The time came to warm up the engine, but my pilot friend didn't show up. Someone had to be in the rear cockpit to operate the ignition switch on my signals while I cranked the big propeller—and it really needed to be an experienced pilot or mechanic. But I was getting desperate, so I finally decided to have my nonpilot friend stand at the rear cockpit to operate the switch for me.

The engine had no primer pump—not even a choke. There were four little brass primer cups with valves on the intake manifold. After putting about a thimbleful of gasoline in each cup, the valves were opened to drain the gas down into the manifold and the valves were then closed. To do all that, it was necessary to stand on one of the wheels to reach the primer cups, and that had to be done separately on each side of the plane. The propeller was then pulled about two revolutions to take the prime into the cylinders. The priming charge would then be repeated to provide fuel for the starting engine.

The man pulling the propeller would get one blade into the proper position and call "SWITCH ON" to the man in the cockpit who would then turn on the magneto switch and answer "SWITCH ON." The propeller would then be briskly pulled through the first compression and the engine should start. If it didn't start, then the man in the cockpit would call "SWITCH OFF." It was then necessary to again get the propeller into the proper position for another pull try. If not successful after two or three attempts, the entire process had to be repeated.

With my nonpilot friend at the pilot's cockpit to work the switch, I started the procedure about 30 minutes before the scheduled poppy drop, none too much time. I cranked the prop and then I cranked it again and again, priming in between. My heart was pounding from the exertion. It looked like it was going to be no-go. I thought of using the smaller Jenny, but with the short time left, I was committed to getting that Hispano engine started.

By 11:04, I was getting weaker, and I had to get that plane into the air by 11:05 to make the drop on schedule. In desperation, I gave it one more swing, then another and suddenly, the engine came to life. I made a dive behind the revolving propeller on my hands and knees and pulled the two chocks from the wheels. The plane started to roll forward, and I rolled on my back as the lower wing passed over me, then I leaped for the rear cockpit as my friend scrambled to get into the front cockpit. There was no time to buckle my seat belt, a warm-up, a magneto check—nothing. It was just GO!

With the engine and its gallons of cooling water stone cold, you can imagine how reluctant it was to respond to the open throttle. (Accelerating pumps had not yet been invented.) The engine burped, snorted and backfired as the plane slowly accelerated, lifted off and barely cleared the trees at the edge of the field.

A necessarily gentle turn toward Poughkeepsie and a bare climb with the engine weakly trying put us on our way just over the treetops. The engine was giving intermittent bursts of power between noisy pops and bangs. I felt naked without my safety belt, but there was no time to let go of the controls to fasten it. I just had to keep the engine running until it was warmed up so we could get some precious altitude. I intercepted Main Street at about 400 feet and finally reached about 700 feet.

About a mile from the target, I had the engine going well, but by then I had to start my fast glide to the target. So I throttled it to idle for the silent approach. I knew I was running late but was much too busy to look at my wristwatch while judging the steep glide—almost a dive.

The prop was windmilling; the wing wires were whistling. Over the nose I could see an enormous crowd in front of City Hall overflowing into Washington Street. As we passed over the target at about 300 feet, I signaled to my friend Russ to toss the poppies. He dumped them into the wind—including the cardboard box itself—and we glided away, a cloud of poppies floating behind us.

At no more than 250 feet, I continued the glide, the throttle almost closed, and proceeded down the grade of Main Street toward the river. When we were about a block past the target, I applied power but got precious little of it because the engine was cold again. It started backfiring with the windmilling propeller turning it. I was descending toward Main Street, getting closer to those 600-volt trolley wires, and still desperately trying to coax more power out of the engine.

Of course, the carburetor had iced up, and there was no carburetor heat on those engines. The only way to get rid of it is to pump the throttle and cause the backfiring to blow the ice out of the carb venturi.

I was just able to keep above the wires with the engine banging and snorting all the way down to the river. I was trying to figure how to get beyond the wires and over the dock to get my plane to the water. It looked like I might barely clear the dock in a stall and then get wet. I could see the spot where we would hit.

We cleared by a few feet and then down toward the water, still with intermittent power. I held the plane barely above the surface in ground effect. Wonderful! Good old ground effect! We were out over the water, only about four feet above it, but getting farther and farther away from shore as I continued trying to coax more power out of the engine. I was determined to save my beautiful airplane. It had taken me six months of hard work to rebuild it from the wreck I had bought. I had no thought at all of the probability of drowning.

Then, all of a sudden, all eight cylinders started firing. I made a slight right turn into the light breeze, passed under the railroad bridge, then a shallow climb to a few hundred feet over the water. Finally, as we turned back to the airport, I got myself calmed down a little. I was shivering from excitement, but I was elated at having saved my airplane. I felt greatly disappointed at having fouled up the poppy drop thing.

As I expected, about an hour after we landed, the big open touring car with the Legionnaires came speeding toward the airport. I figured they were undoubtedly upset with me about my having ruined their carefully laid plan.

The car slid to a stop in a cloud of dust. All four doors swung open and the Legionnaires burst out of it and came running toward me. They jumped all over me, shaking my hands, all talking at once, and enthusiastically *thanking* me for such a perfectly timed "bombing."

They said when the buglers were playing *Taps* and the plane was not heard coming they were disappointed. Then, just as the final notes sounded, the poppies came silently floating down over the crowd of people. It was a complete surprise! Hundreds had tears in their eyes.

They had not heard even the sound of the whistling wires of the biplane over the bugles. They were looking at the buglers and standing at attention, and had not seen the plane pass overhead. Because the plane was a little to the right of Main Street and slightly behind the crowd, the northwest breeze carried the poppies so they drifted right over the heads of the people.

Those Legionnaires could not thank me enough, nor could they understand how I was able to time the drop so well—and so *silently*. Little did they know!

I can still plainly see those 600-volt wires under the wings and the water just under the wheels…

Driving the Governor's Wife

ONE EVENING IN 1928 AS THE SUN WAS SETTING AT THE END OF A PLEASANT SUMMER DAY, WE WERE TYING DOWN OUR OPEN COCKPIT BIPLANES FOR THE NIGHT WHEN A SIX-PLACE TRAVEL AIR 6000 MONOPLANE APPEARED, ONE OF THE VERY LATEST AIRPLANES ON THE MARKET.

Six-place Travel Air 6000 monoplane, new on the market in 1928

The plane circled and made a high fast approach over the tall locust trees toward the swamp at the end of the grass runway. But it was coming in much too fast and too far down the runway, and a go-around was started.

We watched in trembling awe as the plane made a steep left climbing turn, so steep that the wings were rocking close to stalls. A second approach was made, but this time it was not quite as fast as the first and the steep stalling climbout was repeated.

It is difficult to describe those steep-climbing, stalling turns. They were terrifying. We were sure that the plane would stall. Had there been a phone available on the field, we would have called the fire department.

The plane finally did land, tail high but so far down the runway that, even with full braking, it stopped with the wheels on the very edge of the swamp, its engine sticking out over the embankment. We ran over and manually pulled the plane back so the pilot could restart the engine and taxi to a tiedown spot.

The pilot and a lady passenger got out and requested transportation—the pilot to a hotel and the lady to her home near Poughkeepsie. The pilot said he had just bought the plane in Wichita and had stopped en route to pick up the lady passenger.

We said nothing but realized that he obviously did not have sufficient experience to fly that airplane. He commented on the shortness of the field, blaming that for his difficulty in landing. Another almost brand new Travel Air 6000 based on the field was owned by a local man who hired a professional pilot. He had no difficulty landing the 6000 on the field—but we said nothing about that either.

One of the other local pilots took the pilot to a hotel for the night, and I took the lady to her home. During the ride in my Model T Ford, she talked about what a wonderful first flight she had just enjoyed and how enthusiastic she was about flying. Still psychologically shocked from the landing I had witnessed, I just nodded and said nothing.

The next morning, the pilot took off solo to fly to some place in the Carolinas. The following day, we read in the newspaper that after two or three attempts to land, the airplane had crashed and burned, killing the pilot. I still have that news clipping. I suspected he was making his go-arounds without readjusting the stabilizer for climbout, after having adjusted it for landing approach. Thus, there was a tendency to climb out too steeply.

The lady passenger I had driven to her home in Hyde Park was the wife of the governor of New York, Franklin Delano Roosevelt, who probably never knew how close his wife came to death nor how close we came to having a different history of the United States! Ⓜ

21

New Standard D-25

IN 1929 I WAS EMPLOYED BY NORWALK AIRWAYS, A SMALL FIRM IN NORWALK, CONNECTICUT, TO TAKE DELIVERY OF AND FLY THEIR NEWLY PURCHASED NEW STANDARD D-25 FIVE-PLACE BIPLANE. THAT AIRPLANE WAS DESIGNED ESPECIALLY FOR BARNSTORMING AFTER THE DEPARTMENT OF COMMERCE, IN 1927, GROUNDED THE OLD WORLD WAR I STANDARD J-1 WITH HISPANO-SUIZA ENGINES OPERATED BY THE GATES FLYING CIRCUS.

A 1928 New Standard D-25, S/N 2, converted from 180-hp Hispano to 220-hp Wright J-5 with five-place front cockpit, pilot seat in rear.

The New Standard D-25 was designed by an engineer from the Sikorsky organization under the supervision of Charles Healy Day, the designer of the original WWI Standard J-1, and Clyde Pangborn, the chief pilot of the Gates Flying Circus.

The airplane was powered by a Wright J-5 engine of 225 hp, the same type of radial engine that flew Charles Lindbergh across the Atlantic in 1927. The pilot sat in the rear cockpit to balance the engine and the four passengers sat in a large bathtub-shaped cockpit on the center of lift under the upper wing center section, all facing forward. It was an ideal airplane for barnstorming on a large scale, such as the Gates operation—out of grass fields of limited size. A field of 1,000 feet was ample with a full load and no wind.

I took delivery from Clyde Pangborn, who was then chief test pilot for the New Standard Aircraft Corp. at Teterboro Airport, New Jersey. After flying it to Hartford for Connecticut licensing, I took it on to the little hilltop field at Norwalk, its home base, overlooking the city and the harbor and Long Island Sound. The takeoff was slightly downgrade with no obstructions to clear, right out over the city and harbor.

The owners had arranged a

special day to introduce their new $10,000 airplane to the citizens of Norwalk. It was Sunday and there was a big crowd that kept me very busy hopping four passengers at a time at $2.50 a head on very short hops, $10 per load. It was a fast, lucrative operation, so the owners were on their way to paying off the cost of the airplane. I was making a good commission of 28 percent.

The hops were no more than five minutes in the air, just out over the city and harbor and back for a quick reload, out one side of the cockpit and in the other simultaneously with a good pit crew. It was a tight field and landings had to be made precisely. All area around the field was residential. It was three months before the great stock market crash of October 1929 and everyone had money to spend.

Connecticut had the first aviation regulatory laws, originating in 1911. They were really more restrictive in purpose than regulatory, for many wealthy people in the state hated airplanes. Some had actually sued in attempts to prevent flying over their land, claiming it was trespassing. Failing in that effort, they had instigated the regulatory laws and later the aviation commission to enforce them, thus establishing a nice comfortable bureaucracy for some appointees. We pilots used

to call it the "Commission for the Suppression of Aviation," which fit it perfectly.

Even after the Federal Dept. of Commerce Bureau of Aeronautics took over air commerce regulation in 1927, the Connecticut Commission of Aviation actually expanded and proceeded to over-regulate and tax civil aviation. They specified requirements for every airfield, public or private, even small private airstrips and charged fees for their licenses.

All pilots and mechanics had to take state written exams, flight tests and medical exams, duplicates of the federal tests and pay fees for state licenses. Each airplane was inspected by a state inspector and licensed each year for a fee—in addition to a state personal property tax. Any fixed base operation was licensed and taxed. Non-fixed base operation such as barnstorming was therefore not possible. Insurance requirements were burdensome. It was a real paradox that civil aviation could exist at all in the Commonwealth of Connecticut.

There was one state aircraft inspector—I will call him Mr. P., the initial of his name—who had been some pre-WWI early bird's mechanic. He made it known that he was the world's most senior, knowledgeable and strict inspector in

Mr. P. found some small items lying on the seat of a plane of a friend of mine and grounded the airplane because they were not tied down! The owner entered his hangar to go flying, only to find the plane red-tagged.

existence. He was on duty five days a week, but on weekends he would, on his own time, drive around the state and harass the pilots who were trying to make a living.

It is hard to believe some of the stunts that the guy would pull. He had the right under the law to enter a hangar at any time and inspect an airplane and ground it, even without the knowledge of the owner. As an example, he found some small items lying on the seat of a plane of a friend of mine and grounded the airplane because they were not tied down! The owner entered his hangar to go flying, only to find the plane red-tagged.

There was a regulation prohibiting airplanes to be tied down outdoors, except temporarily. That was one of his favorites. Many Connecticut airplane owners kept their planes over in New York State, and many still do to avoid heavy personal property taxes on them, even though most of the harassing state regulations have been rescinded.

Right in the middle of my first Sunday of passenger hopping, sure enough, Mr. P. appeared. Just the previous week he had inspected the airplane, stenciled the state license symbol on its fuselage and collected the annual fee. However, in front of my crowd of eager passenger prospects, he ordered me to stop flying so that he could inspect the airplane again.

He could not find anything wrong with the brand-new plane, but did notice a slight tear in the canvas boot on the tailskid, a little three-quarter-inch tear caused by a stick or stone. He walked around to the propeller, put a red grounding tag on the hub and announced, in front of the crowd, that a new canvas boot would have to be installed and a report made to him before any more flying could be done. This was right in the middle of my first big day of passenger flying! He then loaded his family back into his car and drove away, probably to harass another pilot somewhere.

The purpose of that canvas boot was to exclude dirt and grass, and possibly field mice, from getting up into the fuselage. That little three-

Murphy's Law had not at that time been discovered, Murphy himself not having been born. But it was in effect nonetheless, just as the Law of Gravity before Newton.

cornered tear was not likely to admit much of such. After Mr. P. had gone out of sight—to the delight of the crowd—I tore off the red tag and resumed flying.

The Mayor of Norwalk had been invited to take a flight in the new airplane and in due time he arrived with three other men ready to go. When I saw them, I was shocked: Each one weighed at least 250 pounds, I suspected more. They were enormous. That was somewhat in excess of the 170-pound average passenger weight specified in the airplane's certificate.

The mayor had been told by the owners that the plane could easily take them all at once. I considered the light load of fuel, the slightly downgrade takeoff with no obstructions, the lower terrain ahead and a good breeze—and decided to go. In those days, enforcement of weight allowances was lax. When they got aboard, I could feel the shock struts settle down. But off we went in a cloud of dust.

Murphy's Law had not at that time been discovered, Murphy himself not having been born. But it was in effect nonetheless, just as the Law of Gravity before Newton. So, just as I was lifting off, with all of the field behind me, and I mean no more ahead due to that heavy load, the engine lost power and started shak-

ing the whole airplane violently via the rigid engine mount ring. We launched out over the city in a sinking condition, heading for a dip in the drink of the harbor, if I could make it.

In those days, few single-engine airplanes had airspeed indicators and none had Pilot Operation Handbooks. It was just up to the pilot to familiarize himself with performance, etc. Fortunately, the D-25 was one of the earliest planes to come equipped with an airspeed indicator, and I had experimented with stall and performance speeds, especially best-angle and rate-of-climb speeds, during the ferry flights.

There was no instrumentation, since there was no IFR to speak of at that time. The altimeter was the old non-sensitive type, for today's Kollsman sensitive altimeter had yet to be invented.

As I settled down toward the rooftops, almost following the slope of the terrain, headed for the water, I found one airspeed that stopped the descent and actually gave me a very slight climb, as judged by eye and feel (the pucker factor). I had not gotten low enough to get ground effect, but by holding straight ahead and carefully holding the best airspeed, I was getting just a little climb, heading out over Long Island Sound with smoother air over the water. The engine was holding its lower power and its vibration and extraneous popping and banging was at a steady level.

Oil pressure was OK. Numerous small sailboats out on the sound were reassuring. Without losing any of that precious altitude, I was able to make a very, very gradual downwind turn back inland. Over the land, I felt a slight upward thermal and nicely made it over the rising ground for a downwind leg to the field. I did not risk a 10-12 mph downwind landing back on the field because the field was too short and a crash would have been inevitable and disastrous—especially with the crowd of people at the downwind end.

By very careful attention to airspeed, I was able to make a second turn, clearing the houses by a hundred feet or less and made a power landing that apparently looked perfectly normal to the people on the ground. Due to the long slotted opening in the exhaust pipe, not many people had noticed the irregular exhaust of the engine.

Believe me, I was bushed and just sat in the cockpit trying to look calm and normal while the men debarked. I was thinking of what a disaster had been averted and how I never again would risk such an overload.

My four passengers, however, were all very enthusiastic. They had thoroughly enjoyed their close view of the city from their first airplane flight and seemed perfectly oblivious to my problem—or anything unusual. All four were important men in the community and obviously had no idea that a disaster had been narrowly avoided.

I accepted their compliments and talked to them for a few minutes, trying to conceal my perturbation and swallow my heart, while four new paying passengers were loaded by the ticket sellers. But when the four men were gone, I made an excuse to go to the hangar where I told the owners that flying was definitely over for that day.

Of course, what I wanted to know was what had caused the trouble with the engine. After scratching my head a little for ideas, I felt the cylinders to see which one was misfiring. I was not surprised to discover that three cylinders were cold as clams, evenly spaced around the nine.

Being an A&E mechanic, I then had a hint of the cause. The Wright J-5 engine had a three-barrel carburetor, each barrel feeding three cylinders through independent manifold passageways cast into the rear section of the crankcase.

There were two things that

I did not risk a 10-12 mph downwind landing back on the field because the field was too short and a crash would have been inevitable and disastrous—especially with the crowd of people at the downwind end.

could cause such a cessation of the *three* cylinders fed by one barrel of the carburetor. Of course, the most probable cause would be a particle of dirt in the jet, or some other failure in that section of the carburetor. That was hard for me to determine without taking the carburetor off and would take time in the field. The other possibility would be a sticking intake valve.

So I started taking the valve rocker covers off and in the very first one I found the cause of the severe loss of power and the vibration. There are two concentric valve springs in a J-5 valve action. I was surprised to find *both* springs broken and screwed into themselves, probably a million-to-one occurrence. So the valve was not closing and was allowing that cylinder to backfire into the manifold, cutting out the other two cylinders.

That accounted for the severe vibration and extreme loss of power and the extraneous popping and snorting by the engine, which my passengers evidently thought was

normal. At that time, there were no controllable propellers or governors, so the fixed propeller reduced the rpm and caused still further loss of power, I'm sure fully 60 percent.

Every time I even think of that experience, I can feel the adrenaline flow and my heart take a few extra jumps. Mr. P. never did find out about it. That airspeed indicator certainly paid for itself and made me a devout believer in their value in those days of seat-of-the-pants flying.

Today, I also have an angle-of-attack indicator in my plane, and I truly believe that if they were required equipment, many takeoff climbout and landing approach accidents could be avoided. Ⓜ

My Barnstorming System

I SOLOED IN MY OWN JENNY ON DECEMBER 15, 1923, AND GRADUATED IN MECHANICAL ENGINEERING IN 1927, MIXING FLYING WITH MY STUDIES. THAT YEAR, THE NEW AIR REGULATIONS STARTED AND I QUALIFIED FOR AN A&E #2906.

Since I didn't have funds for another airplane with which to qualify for one of the new pilot certificates, I worked for the Gates Flying Circus as a mechanic. I participated in a few of their events, one of them being at Pittsfield, Massachusetts, in 1927—the biggest weekend in the history of the circus, measured by gross take.

After observing their methods of advertising and publicity, I devised what I thought would be a better way, but I did not reveal my idea. I preferred instead to keep it to myself for my own future use when I had acquired a new plane of my own and could go out barnstorming alone to try it out.

I accumulated money working for Gates and bought the wreck of a WWI Standard J-1—the same type used by the Gates Circus. They had Hispano-Suiza engines of 180 hp, replacing the original Hall-Scott four-cylinder 100-hp engines.

It took me six months of hard work to restore the J-1 to first-class condition and install a Hisso engine. I had planned to carry four passengers in the front cockpit, just as Gates had done, with close to half a million passengers. But one of the new Department of Commerce inspectors told me he would not allow more than two passengers in the front cockpit.

I tried barnstorming with the J-1, but with only half a load it did not pay, so I sold it in 1929. That Standard J-1, with the same engine, still exists and is owned by a man in Yellow Springs, Ohio (as of 2002).

In 1929 the newly designed New Standard D-25 with Wright J-5 225-hp engine was available. It was specifically designed for barnstorming and carried four passengers facing forward in the front open cockpit. I started flying that type and was able to successfully apply my idea of advertising and publicity to get large crowds to part with substantial sums of money for short flights. *Very short.*

Most barnstorming at that time was conducted in the proximity of fairs and carnivals, or at least on established airports or airstrips already used by previous airplanes and where the local population was already familiar with airplanes.

The methods of publicizing the usual weekend events was to use newspaper advertising, printed posters and, of course, whatever stories the local newspapers could be coaxed to print about the event. Often, these were combined with some advertising by local merchants. Of course, one of the major attractions was sometimes an airshow of aerobatic flying, parachute jumps and so on. Those methods were beginning to be outworn in the late 1920s and were no longer very effective.

For barnstorming, the airplane was parked in front of the crowd. A man with a megaphone or PA system would usually talk to the crowd to hawk tickets for flights. When the plane was loaded—with most of its seats filled—the plane would take off and disappear in the distance for 10 to 20 minutes. The big feature of these flights was their length and the sights to be seen from the air.

It was boring to hang around an airport in the hot summer sun to watch such flying. While the plane was out on its cross-country trip, the crowd would lose interest and begin

I had planned to carry four passengers in the front cockpit of the J-1, just as Gates had done, with close to half a million passengers. But one of the new Department of Commerce inspectors told me he would not allow more than two passengers in the front cockpit.

to disperse. If some of those so-called barnstormers grossed $200 to $300 in a day, it was considered to be just fine. The price of a flight was usually at least $5 for a 10-minute flight, or up to as much as $15 for longer rides.

After watching the Gates Flying Circus sell very short rides for only $2.50 per person, four at a time, which were grossing $1,000 or more per day per plane, I could see the possibility of going further with the idea of very short hops at a still lower price—and using my idea of a more effective method of advertising.

Before revealing my advertising method, however, I will describe a necessary and integral part of the whole plan: Preliminary preparations of the fields to be used for the event. For my plan to work, a large enough field was needed to permit landing, stopping to reload and then a take-off—all without wasting any time turning or taxiing. The plane needed to take off right from the place where it stopped to reload, in the same direction without any turning whatever, because fast action would be required to take full advantage of the crowd.

It was necessary to select a field out in the farm country, away from any center of population that would already be familiar with airplanes due to an airport or airstrip nearby. When such a field was found, it would be made suitable for flight operation by

grading, tree removal, blasting of rocks and stumps, and by opening up fences and filling or plank-bridging drainage ditches.

I got to be an expert with dynamite, saws, axes and shovels for there were no chain saws or bulldozers in those days. All of this had to be arranged by contract with the owner and a fee paid for a weekend and usually an option to return for a rain date or repeat date, for another fee.

An iron-bound written agreement was necessary because when the owner would see how much money was taken in, he might be tempted to raise the fee. All this had to be done at least a week in advance of the weekend to be used. A location of this kind—away from any previous flying operation—was called virgin territory and it was very important, but not difficult, to find at that time.

If there was room for parking of cars, a gate had to be made for them and a parking area defined and marked off. Otherwise, the parking had to be on the adjacent road, which would, of course, be quite a distance in each direction and require spectators to walk. No special permits were required in those days, but sometimes the state police would get rather upset about all those cars parked along the road, which they claimed were a detriment to traffic.

A barnstorming poster John used in 1931.

The penny postal cards were the very reason for the great success of my barnstorming 70 years ago. This is the only original one I have left.

Everyone else was very happy.

At least a week in advance, a trip was made by automobile to each village post office in a 10- to 20-mile radius, in inverse proportion to the density of the farm population—a matter of experienced judgment.

Penny postal cards were purchased at each of the post offices to twice the total number in the village and RFD boxes serviced by that post office, and a record was kept of the number at each. It was very important to buy the postal cards at the very same post office from which they were to be mailed because the post office got credit for the volume of sales. It was also necessary to keep the postmaster and carriers happy for all the extra work they were going to do for us.

The cards purchased at each post office were kept in bundles and marked. They were then taken to a local village printer where they were printed on the blank side with the advertising and on the address side with "Box Holder" and the name of the post office for each group of cards. This caused extra work for the printer because he had to change the type for each group. All of this procedure was important to the success of my plan.

When the cards were all printed and in separate groups each was divided in two separate bundles to be mailed on two successive days.

It would be explained to the post-master that it was very important to deliver the first half of them on Thursday and the second half on Friday. Each family would get two cards just before the weekend.

They advertised flights for only $1 per person in a wonderful new $10,000 airplane with a Wright Whirlwind engine, (the same kind that flew Charles Lindbergh across the Atlantic Ocean in 1927). Stunt flying, dead-engine landings and sometimes a parachute jump were sometimes also offered.

Arrows printed on cardboard with "FLY $1" were posted on poles and trees on the surrounding roads to guide the cars to the field. Posters were sometimes used but not at all important. The postal cards did it all.

At the field, steel posts were driven into the ground in a long line parallel to the landing area and half-inch ropes strung along them to keep the crowd back. The posts and the ropes also formed a corral area behind the fence for people who had purchased tickets.

A "chute" area was formed outward from the fence line to hold four passengers for the next flight. Chains were used as gates for the corral and chute. This was all very important for the fast action that would take place.

New Standard biplane being refueled with the engine running. John is standing up in the cockpit, ready to go.

A local gasoline station was offered the privilege of having its logo painted on the side of the fuselage of the plane with washable watercolors in return for delivering two or three drums of Good Gulf or Texaco auto gasoline and some cans of engine oil to the field for free. It never failed and the stations advertised that their gasoline and oil must be good stuff if it worked in a Whirlwind. They often painted their names on the drums. We absolutely never bought any gas.

When those cards arrived at each farm or village home, they caused lots of excitement, especially among the children who would urge the parents to take them on Saturday or Sunday. As soon as the milking and feeding was done, the family would pile into the Model T and rush to the field, following the arrows and holding the cards. Farm families get up early, so they started arriving after daylight and action began.

A good pit crew was necessary. It consisted of a ticket-seller, a man to load the four passengers and another man to simultaneously unload the previous four on the opposite side of the plane. These two loader/unloader men were also trained to refuel the plane from five-gallon cans and a funnel *with the engine running* to save time.

The plane was flown with a light fuel load, so now and then another five gallons of gas was put in. One man would climb up the steps on the landing gear shock strut to stand on the cowling over the engine behind the revolving propeller. The other man would pass up the funnel and gas can. For safety, it was all done very quickly before the next passengers got in.

The sequence of action went like this: The loading man would have four passengers ready in the chute, and as soon as the wing of the plane passed the chute, he would drop the chain and urge them to run to the plane and start climbing up on the lower wing and into the cockpit that was already being vacated by the previous passengers—urged by the unloading man who had been wait-

A gasoline station was offered the privilege of having its logo painted on the fuselage in return for delivering two or three free drums of auto gasoline and cans of engine oil to the field.

It was a real roller-coaster kind of a ride and the people loved it. They all got out laughing and many went right back for a second ride.

ing outside of the spot where the plane would stop.

He would run in behind the wing and urge the four previous passengers to get out and climb down. He would get them far enough away to let the tail of the plane pass them. The next takeoff was begun just as soon as they were out of the way of the tail—often before the new load of passengers had even seated themselves. Because the ride was so short, passengers usually did not get their belts on before they were back on the ground again.

The unloading man would then guide the previous passengers back to a gate into the crowd area, then take up his post again. The loading man would get four new passengers together from the corral to go on the next flight. By that time, about a minute after takeoff, all would be ready for the next load/unload sequence.

The flights were very short, about one minute block-to-block. And though you may find it hard to believe, about 50 flights in an hour could be made. That was $200 per hour! The flying would begin early and last until dark—"dew to dew," as a harvester would say. And we were really harvesting the greenbacks, all gold in those days. It was easy to make 250 to 350 flights in a day—$1,000 to $1,400 in revenue.

The engine never stopped all day and I never got out of the cockpit. I made my own relief tube and still have the little funnel I hammered out of copper to connect to a hose. I ate, drank and "undrank" right in the cockpit. I enjoyed it and never tired. It was really fun making all that money.

Here's how we could make such short flights: The takeoff began right at the chute. After liftoff, the plane was held down two or three seconds and then lifted up into a steep climbing 180-degree turn to downwind, a cross between a wingover and an Immelmann*. Shortly after passing the touchdown area, a steep banked turn was made to land. The speed was killed by very wide fishtailing and touchdown was made exactly on the same spot each time so that the plane could be slightly braked to a stop with the lower wing just past the chute.

It was a real roller-coaster kind of a ride and the people loved it. They all got out laughing and many went right back and bought tickets for a second ride. I was aware people who had never been close to an airplane before just wanted a short sample ride the first time—not a long one. A family of four could go up for $4, far less than $20 or more that it would cost at an airport. None complained.

With the airplane going up and down like fury and never a break, the excitement was high. People who would normally not take a chance on flying got caught up in the enthusiasm and did it—by the hundreds. The tailskid would actually dig a big hole in the ground where it touched down repeatedly in an area of only five or six feet.

The flying would become almost automatic from repetition. In the evening, it was fun to lay out all that money on the beds and the floor of the hotel room to count it and check the tickets against it, and then divide it up. Even though it was obvious to many people that we were loaded with money at the end of the day, there was little chance of a holdup in those days. Nevertheless, I always carried a .32 Colt pistol.

None of the other pilots ever learned about my method and I did not brag about how many passengers I carried because they might get curious and investigate. They were all busy on some airport trying to get people to part with five bucks for a 10 or 15 minute ride, so they did not know what I was doing or where I was.

It was often several weeks before I would even touch down on an established airport because I was always out in the farm country somewhere. The men who worked for me were not aviation people so they did not go to airports. In fact, I kept them busy seven days a week. So this is the first time I have revealed or written about my method.

I like to think about the thousands of people who flew with me on their very first flights before the era of airlines more than 60 years ago when airplanes were still open cockpit biplanes. They are the airline passengers of today.

In later years, when I was flying the airliners, I often wondered if any of the people I introduced to flying might be riding with me in a pressurized jet airliner at 35,000 feet—but I was afraid to ask.

My copilots—and even the flight attendants—sometimes asked how I could make such consistently good landings. I just told them I'd had a "helluvalotta" practice while barnstorming—like 250 or more landings a day! Ⓜ

* *Immelmann (turn): A maneuver in which an airplane is half looped to an upside-down position and then half rolled back to normal, upright flight: used to gain altitude while reversing direction: named after German ace M. Immelmann (1890-1916).*

A Narrow Escape

THE D-25 BIPLANE HAS AN OPEN COCKPIT WITH THE PILOT SEATED IN THE REAR AND A LARGE FOUR-PLACE PASSENGER SEATING ARRANGEMENT UP FRONT. ALTHOUGH IT WAS DESIGNED SPECIFICALLY FOR BARNSTORMING AND HOPPING PASSENGERS, BOOTLEGGERS IN THE UNITED STATES FOUND IT IDEAL FOR SMUGGLING LOADS OF AS MUCH AS 1,000 POUNDS OF WHISKEY FROM CANADA.

In December 1929, I was flying a New Standard D-25 on the first Florida Air Tour. The air tour started following the first Miami Air Race and went to about 40 cities in Florida with about 40 planes. I was hopping passengers at each stopover.

The stopover at St. Petersburg was at the airport—right between the dock on Tampa Bay and the edge of the central part of the city. It was only a short walk from the plane to the hotel. The edge of the airport, which seemed like a dock to me, consisted of heavy timbers with the level of the field perhaps six to eight feet above the water level.

While standing at the edge of the dock, my mechanic and I could see numerous barracuda in the water and we amused ourselves by throwing fish heads to them. It was obvious these fish were accustomed to being tossed food treats as they were very adept at anticipating where the fish heads would strike the water, and a number of them would converge at that spot. The competition was frantic as they grabbed for them.

Barracuda are fierce creatures with rows of razor-sharp teeth and streamlined bodies that make them reputedly the fastest fish in the sea. As we watched them roiling the water as they scrambled for fish heads, we speculated about how unhealthy it would be to make a forced landing in the bay after taking off from that waterfront airport.

A short time later we took off right over the spot where we had been feeding the barracuda. Our big front cockpit was loaded with the mechanic along with quantities of spare parts, tools and much other equipment for our barnstorming tour, including a big bundle of steel fence posts and a sledgehammer for driving them. Certainly overloaded.

As I lifted the plane over the barracudas' feeding area, I was aware of the danger. But as usual, I just didn't let it worry me. I had performed a good preflight and had checked the engine and the magnetos before beginning the takeoff.

As I started a steep climb in the haze, I suddenly saw a rain shower moving directly toward me. There was a distinct sharp wall of rain I could not avoid, and we flew right into it. Instantly, the engine quit cold about 500 feet above the water!

As a very experienced airshow aerobatic pilot, in a split second I instinctively made a sharp left bank and dive for an immediate course reversal to return to the dock and a downwind landing over those hungry barracuda.

As I rapidly approached the big, solid wood timbers at the edge of the water, I saw I was not going to make it. My wheels would strike the timbers! In the last split second before they hit, I lifted the nose just

While standing at the edge of the dock, my mechanic and I could see numerous barracuda in the water and we amused ourselves by throwing fish heads to them…As we watched them roiling the water as they scrambled for fish heads, we speculated about how unhealthy it would be to make a forced landing in the bay…

Now why, we wondered, did that wonderful, reliable Wright J-5 engine that had carried Lindbergh safely across the Atlantic decide to quit just at that most inconvenient time?

enough to put the wheels on the edge of the dock and quickly shoved the stick forward to get the tail skid over, too. With the help of the tailwind, we had made it and rolled to a stop.

We sat there, drenched with rain, waiting for our hearts to slow down, thankful for our good luck. Now why, we wondered, did that wonderful, reliable Wright J-5 engine that had carried Lindbergh safely across the Atlantic decide to quit just at that most inconvenient time?

The answer was very simple. The two good Scintilla magnetos on a J-5 engine are not *behind* the engine but right out front, exposed to the rain. In that airplane, no cowling had been provided to shield them from the rain. So when the water hit them, they quit cold. You can be sure that I had cowling made for them without delay.

Some time later, when I was operating an aircraft shop at Poughkeepsie, I rebuilt a damaged Bellanca CH-300 for a customer who was using the airplane to smuggle whiskey over the Canadian border. I had also given the 300-hp engine a top overhaul. The wings were covered with new fabric also. At least two other bootleggers' airplanes were in the shop. They were competitors of each other and of the Bellanca owner.

Dean Ivan Lamb, the pilot who came to take delivery, was a very expert and experienced aerobatic-savvy aviator. As he reached an altitude of about 500 feet after a very steep climb—due to no load—the engine quit cold without warning. I watched as he did the very same thing I had done at St. Petersburg: He returned to the field safely and landed down-wind.

In most cases, it is unsafe to turn around for return to the airport after an engine quits on takeoff climbout. But under some circumstances, an experienced pilot can do it by making a quick, steeply banked, short dive for a 180-turn.

Of course, I was worried that maybe I had done something wrong while performing the top overhaul of the engine. But it turned out that sometime during the night, while the airplane was in the hangar, a competing pilot had poured into the fuel tanks a combination of floor sweepings containing dust, wood chips, sawdust, sand and even tacks and small brads. We had to cut open the brand new fabric to remove the tanks and cut them open, too, for cleaning. Ⓜ

Search in a Storm

I N THE WINTER OF 1929-1930, I WAS BARNSTORMING IN A D-25 BIPLANE WITH A WRIGHT J-5, 225-HP ENGINE, AND WAS STAYING IN MOBILE, ALABAMA, FOR A FEW DAYS DURING A STORM, WHICH WAS EITHER AN ACTUAL HURRICANE OR CLOSE TO IT. THERE WAS A SUSTAINED, VERY HIGH AND GUSTY WIND WITH DRIVING RAIN. I HAD MY AIRPLANE TIED DOWN ON THE ONLY AIRPORT THERE AT THE TIME, A GRASS FIELD RIGHT NEXT TO THE WEST SHORE OF MOBILE BAY, SITE OF THE FAMOUS CIVIL WAR BATTLE.

Trees about 50 feet high lined the shore between the field and the water of the bay. I was at the airport to make sure my airplane did not blow away in the high wind, when a man came to me requesting that I fly over the bay to search for his young son and another boy. They had set out in a small open motorboat to sail from New Orleans to Mobile and their arrival was long overdue.

At that time there were no TV satellite depictions of weather, so the storm had struck without any warning. The father was frantic. He said the Coast Guard had been searching for the boat on its route along the north side of the Gulf of Mexico with no success. The Coast Guard did not have airplanes, so they were searching with a small C.G. Cutter, leaving a search of the bay until later.

The father had decided the boys had probably progressed far enough east to be in Mobile Bay by that time, where the Guard was not yet searching. It was chilly weather for Mobile. The wind and waves on the bay were really far too violent for any small boat, especially an open in-board motorboat. I could see the churning water from the airport; conditions were positively forbidding and definitely dangerous. With a very low ceiling of about 60 feet, getting over the 50-foot trees looked impossible in the gusty east wind and heavy rain.

At first I declined to fly at all, but then I felt sorry for the father and, of course, for the two boys. Finally, against my better judgment I decided to try, and my mechanic

John Miller in 1930 with his New Standard D-25, an open cockpit five-place biplane with Wright J-5 225-hp engine.

helper consented to go with me as an observer. Both he and I realized that I would be so busy merely flying the airplane under that very low ceiling in fog, heavy rain and high gusty wind that I could not do much searching over the water while flying in those conditions.

We had no radio and no life-saving equipment whatever. If we hit the water, it would be fatal. Whitecaps of at least four feet were extremely dangerous conditions for a small open boat. With visibility at less than half a mile, I knew I had a tough job ahead of me. I told the father I would charge him $60 an hour for my flying time, but I could not promise success.

I took off toward the trees, barely skimming the tops of them. The water under the plane was really wild. Rain was pounding the little windshield in front of the open cockpit. Any attempt to stick my head into the slipstream was painful to my face and clouded my goggles.

I headed east, out of sight of land until I could see the eastern shore and then started a right turn to head back west, with the inside wing almost touching the water and the outside wing cutting into the low clouds. It was a really wild ride with those vicious waves just below the wingtip in 45-degree banks, giving me false sensations of drifting.

I had to fly the turns by feel to avoid slipping due to the waves moving under me. To cover the entire bay, we flew back and forth from one side to the other, each time covering an area farther south.

Just as I was running out of hope, we found the tiny boat at the south end of the bay. It was barely afloat and the two boys were frantically bailing water, one with his bare hands! With the boat flooded, the inboard engine was dead, of course. The boat was being tossed about with water sloshing around in it.

I could see no life preservers on the boys as I circled overhead. They were so busy bailing water they could not even take time out to wave at us as we circled, our wings barely above water.

I headed north along the west shore until I saw the trees along the airport, then made a circle out over the water to get headed directly toward the trees, hopped over them, again scraping through the bottom of the overcast, downwind and across the field at high speed. As I passed west of the airport, I made a 180 barely over the trees and landed east on the grass. The airplane did not roll a hundred feet in that wind, with power on. What a ride!

The father paid me the $60 for my 60 minutes and rushed off to find a telephone to call the Coast Guard. They were about the hardest dollars I have ever earned.

I never heard a word from the father or the boys. I learned later that the boys were rescued by a private boat. The Coast Guard was still out on the Gulf where conditions must have been much worse.

A few days after that, I flew over the Mobile annual Mardi Gras night parade with fireworks streaming from my airplane. Lotsa fun! Ⓜ

Clyde Pangborn

IN 1931, CLYDE PANGBORN WAS THE FIRST PILOT TO FLY NONSTOP ACROSS THE PACIFIC OCEAN FROM JAPAN TO THE UNITED STATES. AFTER 41 HOURS IN THE AIR, HE LANDED IN HIS HOMETOWN OF WENATCHEE, WASHINGTON. THE TOWN WAS SO PROUD OF HIM, THEY NAMED THEIR AIRPORT CLYDE PANGBORN MEMORIAL AIRPORT.

Clyde was trained in flying during World War I, but not in time to see combat. After discharge he went barnstorming around the country, first in a surplus Jenny, then a J-1 Standard. He and Ivan R. Gates established the famous Gates Flying Circus.

The circus was brought to New York City by the *Daily News*, before there were any air regulations. WWI pilots performed their wild acts right down over Broadway with aerobatics, wing walking and even a plane change down between the buildings, including at Times Square. It was a spectacular show, right over the huge crowds. In 1927 I worked briefly for the circus as a mechanic and became very well-acquainted with Upside-Down Pangborn.

In 1931 Pang and his friend Hugh Herndon started an around-the-world flight in a Bellanca monoplane fitted with a streamlined belly fuel tank. I watched them take off at Floyd Bennett Field in Brooklyn, New York, with a full tank for a nonstop flight to England. They got around the world as far as Japan where they were arrested for having a small camera in the airplane, delaying their attempt to better the standing record of a previous flight. So, they decided to compete for the prize offered for the first nonstop flight from Japan to the U.S.

Later, when I was applying for a job as a pilot for United Air Lines, Pang wrote a letter of recommendation for me in which he stated that I was a "superb pilot." I got the job.

Pang and Roscoe Turner teamed up in 1934 to compete in the big London to Sydney, Australia Air Race. They placed second. The UAL Boeing 247-D they flew in that race is now displayed below and behind the Eastern Air Lines DC-3 in the Smithsonian Air & Space Museum in Washington, D.C.

During WWII Pang flew bombers to deliver them to England, making quite a number of such trips. Sadly, he died, too early, in 1958 of pneumonia.

Whenever you fly to Japan in a jet, remember pioneers Howard Stark and Clyde Pangborn, whose accomplishments were extremely important to aviation in those pioneer days and right to the present.

Here I am a veteran pilot with more than 75 years of flying behind me and still more ahead of me—but Howard Stark, Charles A. Lindbergh and Clyde Pangborn are my civilian pilot heroes. Ⓜ

Clyde Pangborn

Running up the engine of the autogiro at the National Air Races, Los Angeles Mines Field, (now LAX) 1933

First Transcontinental Autogiro

BACK IN 1923 WHEN I WAS IN THE THIRD YEAR OF HIGH SCHOOL—SHORTLY BEFORE I HAD SOLOED IN A JENNY—I READ THE ACCOUNT OF THE FIRST FLIGHTS MADE BY JUAN DE LA CIERVA AT MADRID, SPAIN, IN AN EXPERIMENTAL ROTARY-WING FLYING MACHINE. I WAS ALREADY AWARE THAT HE WAS AN AERONAUTICAL ENGINEER AND HAD BEEN EXPERIMENTING WITH HELICOPTERS. I WAS VERY INTERESTED IN THE HELICOPTER DEVELOPMENT PROBLEM SINCE READING ABOUT THE DE BOTHEZAT HELICOPTER EXPERIMENTS AT MCCOOK FIELD IN 1922, IN *AERIAL AGE MAGAZINE*.

I wrote to Cierva and asked him for details because the newspaper reports had called his aircraft an autogiro. My letter was handwritten in English, and I only half-expected to get a reply. To my surprise, a handwritten reply did come and in perfect English, which he knew even better than I, having been educated at Oxford.

This busy man actually took the time to write to an American schoolboy twice, explaining his autogiro in detail, including its aerodynamics and its possible development into a future helicopter. In those days, many engineers considered the idea of helicopters to be too visionary and crackpot, and it was not even respectable to be associated with such work. This very same attitude had existed relative to heavier-than-air flying machine attempts before the success of the Wrights. In that respect, I was a nonconformist, so I was interested.

By 1931 I had an engineering education and some seven years of successful flying behind me. Harold R. Pitcairn, via his Autogiro Company of America, had become a licensee of the Cierva patents in this country. He had developed a very fine autogiro, the PCA-2, in the factory at Willow Grove, Pennsylvania, where he had manufactured the famous Pitcairn Mailwing airplanes.

The PCA-2s were being ordered by some large corporations to be used for publicity campaigns. The first one sold went to the *Detroit News* and is now in the Ford Museum in Dearborn, Michigan. Another went to Champion to advertise their spark plugs and is the only one still flying. It has been restored by Mr. Pitcairn's son, Steven, and his autogiro-knowledgeable employee, George Townson.

I was the first individual to purchase a PCA-2 for which I paid $15,000—plus a little extra for an auxiliary fuel tank and emergency flare racks for night flying. Delivery for S/N 12 was set for May 1, 1931, but I was later informed that it would be delayed until mid-May. In the meantime, I had planned to make a transcontinental flight to be the first by an autogiro and later a series of exhibition appearances. Pitcairn's sales manager was fully informed of my plans.

Shortly after the first of May, however, I read in the *New York Times* that Amelia Earhart had made an official altitude record for autogiros of 18,000 feet in one of the factory PCA-2s. That height had been exceeded in test flights, but her flight was FAI-NAA observed, so it was official. Before safe oxygen systems existed, that was about as high as it was wise to go without oxygen.

In addition, the *Times* reported that the Beechnut Company was purchasing an autogiro and that Earhart was to make the first transcontinental flight with it.

I quickly flew to Willow Grove to investigate. As I suspected, the sales manager had deliberately inserted the Beechnut order ahead of the delivery of mine, S/N 12. I had been completely familiar with the lineup of earlier serial numbers and when I ordered mine, there had been none ordered by Beechnut.

The Beechnut autogiro was scheduled to be delivered just ahead of mine. The nameplates had been switched so that mine was now S/N 13 and the Beechnut was S/N 12. Due to quiet questions, the mechanics and the test pilots leaked the information to me that the sales manager had decided that he would rather have Earhart make the first transcontinental flight for better publicity coverage, since Beechnut had a large public relations organization, whereas I was a lone professional pilot without such backup. In addition, Earhart had objected to the Serial Number 13, so they obligingly switched number plates.

I was delighted to have S/N 13, just as long as I got my giro first. Earhart had been given just enough instructions to fly the autogiro "airplane-style" so she could make the altitude record. But the factory pilots were having difficulty teaching her how to fly it properly autogiro-style, that is, with vertical descents and landings.

Amelia still was not checked out. I put the sales manager off-guard by telling him that since Amelia was to make a transcontinental flight with the financial backing of Beechnut, I would abandon my plan and simply fly out to Omaha, Nebraska, to fulfill a contract to appear at the Omaha Air Races.

While waiting for delivery of my autogiro, I had been given a checkride by factory test pilot John Lukens in the factory's experimental PCA-1B *Black Maria*, tail number X96N. My logbook shows that he turned me loose after five landings and then during four days, May 9-12, the factory put the aircraft at my disposal for solo practice. My log shows 110 landings for a total of 5.5 hours, averaging only three minutes per flight and including several minutes practice in the clouds with the turn indicator.

I had the advantage of an engineering education and much discussion with factory pilots Jim Ray, John Lukens and Jim Faulkner and the engineers, including chief engineer Agnew Larsen. They told me Amelia showed little understanding or interest in the aerodynamics or mechanics of the autogiro.

My PCA-2, NC10781, S/N 13, was turned over to me at the Pitcairn factory at Willow Grove on the afternoon of May 14. After five short test hops, I took off on the trip to Omaha and on out to California. It was a brand-new engine and brand-new aircraft of radical type, and I naturally had some thoughts of how it might stand up on such a long tour so far away from the factory.

I would often look up at the rotor hub and the spinning blades and wonder just how they were doing, for my life depended on them. No one had ever made such a long trip in a rotary-wing aircraft and, of course, not over such a variety of territory—mountains and deserts included.

It took a few hours to get used to the shadows of the blades passing over me. Sometimes I would hear noises that I had not been aware of before that would make me wonder. At every refueling stop, I carefully inspected the rotor and lubricated the hinge pins. It was a really fine

aircraft and performed beautifully hour after hour, just like a good airplane.

Fortunately, the weather was very good over most of the route. The normal cruising speed was 100 mph, but I cruised at 90 mph—partly to be easy on the new engine and partly to conserve fuel. At that speed, fuel at 18 gph, total duration was only three hours plus about a quarter-hour reserve. If high-octane fuel, high compression, exhaust gas temperature and fuel injection systems had been available at that time, I am sure fuel economy could have been better.

I flew at fairly low altitude most of the time to keep below headwinds. There was no radio communication or navigation, no established airways or traffic control and very little weather information other than on a few air mail routes. There were Department of Agriculture weather bureaus in the larger cities that could be reached by telephone, but they were of precious little, if any, use to pilots— no winds aloft and only hopeful forecasts of good or bad weather. Air mass and frontal information had not yet been discovered in this country.

In those days, a pilot would look at the sky and decide whether to take off. He would then fly until coming to bad weather and if he could get under it, would continue to fly until

it got too low. He would then land, whether or not there was an airfield. Pilotage was navigation by magnetic compass and a pencil line on a chart.

The Rand McNally state maps—which only showed railroads, mountains, lakes, rivers, cities and railroad towns—were the only charts available to me except for some strip charts printed by the Army Air Service between their fields. These were the forebears of the fine sectional charts of today. The Rand McNally maps had known airports, elevations and compass isogonal lines printed in red. So it was easy in daylight to fly accurate courses via pencil lines by magnetic compass, checking the few landmarks shown.

All airports were sod. I had to avoid rain at all costs because it would quickly cut through the fabric on the leading edges of the blades. In an open-cockpit aircraft, all charts had to be marked and folded in advance and packed to avoid having them blow overboard. It was very difficult to spread out a map in such wind.

I was an experienced professional pilot, so navigation was routine and very accurate along the pencil lines. A case in point:

The second day out from Willow Grove (Harrisburg, Pennsylvania, to Chicago, Illinois), after having taken off before daylight, I was arriving after dark after having flown seven hops for a total of 11.3 hours on a route I had never flown before.

In those days, there were no good up-to-date airport directories and I did not know that the Maywood Air Mail Field had been abandoned and a new airport had been built, now known as Chicago Midway. It was not shown on my Rand McNally map.

I continued my exact magnetic compass heading in the dark and estimated exact time to be over the darkened field. Its runway was barely visible in the pitch dark and I landed on it without roll, learned of the new airport and flew to it.

Since the autogiro had no electrical system, there were no landing lights and no instrument lights. The instruments had the old radiant glowing numbers (no longer used, I'm sorry to say), so my eyes were accustomed to the dark and could discern the darkened runway. The position lights were operated by a Hotshot six-volt dry-cell battery only when near an airport, to save the battery (a bit illegal). There was no radio and no control tower.

Since I had to get to Omaha on time, I napped on a workbench and took off without breakfast at daylight. I then flew seven hops and 7.2 hours to Omaha. After arrival, I did two more hours of flying in 14 demonstration hops, same day.

I have nothing but praise for the performance and reliability of the PCA-2 autogiro on that trip and for years afterward.

The trip was southwest to El Paso, Texas, then west. Due to the amount of publicity about the new "windmill airplane," at several of my refueling stops the schools were closed so the children and many others could go see the autogiro.

The day after arrival at the San Diego Naval Air Station on May 29, I made six demonstration flights, including one to take two admirals—Reeves and Stanley—up together for a hop. While they were in the cockpit and I was revving up the rotor for takeoff, a piece of one tooth of the rotor spinning pinion broke off and the greasy fragment dropped down on the uniform trouser of one of the admirals. I forget which one. Of course, I was very embarrassed—especially since I was a mere 2nd Leiutenant, USMCR. I assured them that it did not make any difference to safety and proceeded with the flight.

That morning the Standard Oil Company of California flew their huge Boeing 80-A tri-engine biplane from San Francisco to see the autogiro, and had their logo painted on its side. That same afternoon, I

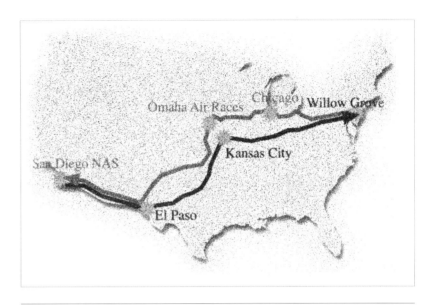

In those days, there were no good up-to-date airport directories and I did not know that the Maywood Air Mail Field had been abandoned and a new airport had been built, now known as Chicago Midway. It was not shown on my Rand McNally map.

flew to Los Angeles and landed at Mines Field (now Los Angeles International Airport, LAX), taking as passenger T. Claude Ryan. A big crowd was waiting at Mines. I made two flights for newsreels, 108-passenger flights, including a return to San Diego, and another round trip to L.A. during the next three days.

At Los Angeles, I was the honored guest at the Hollywood Breakfast Club and sat between two very famous actresses. Mary Pickford was one but I do not remember the other one. I was actually rather embarrassed attending in my flying clothes while everyone else was dressed for the occasion.

The return trip started on June 21. I had a contract to make demonstration flights on the 25th through the 27th at Kansas City Airport. The trip resumed on June 29, landing back at the factory at

John Miller with Admirals Reeves and Stanley, San Diego Naval Air Station

Willow Grove on June 31, where the autogiro received a thorough inspection. All it needed was an oil change!

The Pitcairn PCA-2 was an absolutely fabulous aircraft. It proved so for hundreds of hours of flying afterwards, including aerobatic exhibition flying at the National Air Races, Cleveland, Los Angeles and Chicago, plus a number of other air shows. These aerobatic flights included loops, roll on top of loop and many others, including double Immelmanns starting at grass level.

There was great suspicion among fixed-wing pilots, mechanics and engineers about the strength of the rotor. My aerobatics allayed such suspicions and no such problems ever developed.

After returning from the round trip to California, I offered to appear and loop the autogiro at the 1931 National Air Races in Cleveland, Ohio. Cliff Henderson, the man who ran the National Air Races, was advised by the Pitcairn factory that it would not be possible for me to do it without probable fatal result, so he turned me down.

Pitcairn pilots Jim Ray and Jim Faulkner were there with PCA-2s,

plus a PCA-3 version that had a Pratt & Whitney engine flown by a P&W pilot. Unfortunately, the latter caught fire and burned before the races started due to carburetor flooding during engine start. Lon Yancey was there with the Champion Spark Plug PCA-2 that is now, as I said previously, restored and owned by Steve Pitcairn. It was probably the largest flock of "infuriated palm trees" ever. I did ordinary flying during the races that year and decided to wait until 1932 and try again.

Actually, I had never done a public loop before but had saved the first one for the National Air Races. I had done numerous wingovers which were so inverted that they were almost a loop, and many observers on the ground considered them to be loops. I knew I could do a perfectly straight loop at any time, for I was a very experienced aerobatic pilot.

Pitcairn pilots Jim Ray, Jim Faulkner and John Lukens all told me they had been forbidden to try a loop, but that another pilot had done a maneuver at the factory that was so inverted it was considered to be a loop. They had some doubts that it would pass muster in an aerobatic contest.

In 1932, I joined a traveling air show, The American AirAces, and performed at a number of their shows in the North Central states. I refused to do a straight loop, because I wanted to save the first public one for the National Air Races. I kept my inverted wingovers at least 30 degrees from level at the top and about 45 degrees different direction between entries and departures.

Cliff Henderson agreed to contract with me to perform at the National in Cleveland in 1932. The Pitcairn factory had requested the Department of Commerce Aeronautics Branch to intervene, but they did not have the authority at that time. So the factory requested me to bring the PCA-2 in for a very thorough inspection. I agreed when they promised to have it ready in time. They very kindly loaned me a smaller PAA-1 autogiro so I could visit home in Poughkeepsie while the inspection was performed.

They fulfilled their promise, and I do not in the least blame them for objecting to the aerobatic performances. But I think I did a lot of good for rotary-wing aircraft by demonstrating the safety of the rotors, because most pilots were extremely skeptical about them.

The National Air Races lasted for nine days, including two weekends, and I agreed to a daily performance including loops. Many of my shows are probably in the archives of the newsreel companies' films.

At later air shows, including the 1933 Los Angeles National Air Races and the International Air Races in Chicago, I performed many loops and added a roll on top of a loop and also double Immelmanns starting at grass level. I crisscrossed the United States for the shows.

In addition, I did many hours of banner towing. During one of these, I had one sudden engine stoppage due to a slipped valve timing and landed without damage in a cemetery—the Holy Cross Cemetery in North Arlington, New Jersey, on January 26, 1934. Did not chip a gravestone. It's hard to beat an autogiro for safety.

After I went to work for United Air Lines, my autogiro was sold to a crop-dusting outfit and was destroyed by a hurricane in Florida. A sad end for a noble aircraft. It was the most trouble-free aircraft I have ever flown.

I consider the Pitcairn PCA-2 autogiro, the smaller PAA-1 and PA-18 and the Pitcairn cabin autogiro to be the only *inherently* safe aircraft ever built. ⒨

May 29, 1931: John Miller in his PCA-2 S/N 13 flying over San Diego Naval Air Station the day after arrival. Pictured on the ground are Standard Oil of California's Boeing 80-A tri-motor that flew down from San Francisco and the Ryan Monoplane flown over from San Diego by T. Claude Ryan to see the autogiro.

1931: Omaha Air Races

IT WAS A BEAUTIFUL DAY FOR FLYING AT THE OMAHA AIR RACES IN MAY 1931. DOROTHY HESTER WAS UP IN THE BLUE SKY IN HER LITTLE GREAT LAKES BIPLANE MAKING A WORLD RECORD OF 70 OR MORE OUTSIDE LOOPS. THE RACING PLANES WERE BUSILY BUZZING AROUND THE CLOSED COURSE.

The noise is ear-splitting as the plane passes close to the grandstand by less than 100 feet with its fixed-pitch propeller over-revving. Too close!

Thousands of people were in the grandstand, facing north away from the sun and craning their necks alternately between the air racers flying by and Dorothy—a sparkling, tumbling speck in the sky.

Jimmy Doolittle was sitting on the edge of the cockpit of his Shell Oil Co. Lockheed Sirius low-wing monoplane, one of the most modern and fastest airplanes of the day. He was parked just beyond the east end of the grandstand, facing north, waiting his turn to demonstrate it to the crowd.

Likewise, I was sitting on the edge of the cockpit of my Pitcairn PCA-2 autogiro, just to the right of Doolittle's Sirius. I had taken delivery of the new autogiro only three days before at the Pitcairn factory at Willow Grove near Philadelphia. I immediately started on the first transcontinental flight of a rotary-wing aircraft, picking up an appearance contact at Omaha on the way.

Between the races, the aerobatic pilots were putting on their noisy shows, diving back and forth in front of the grandstand. In contrast, no one could even hear Dorothy or the incomparable Freddie Lund who was effortlessly doing smooth aerobatics in his Taperwing Waco. It was a great setting for fun and excitement.

Suddenly, during a lull in the activities, a beautiful Laird Speedwing biplane with 300-hp Wright engine taxies out about 75 yards and stops, and the engine stops, too. A stream of gasoline gushes out of the bottom of the Laird as the pilot, still in the cockpit, pulls open the dump valve in the long-range tank that filled the front cockpit.

Two men rush out and push the airplane 80 or 100 feet ahead of the gasoline-soaked spot. The engine starts again and the pilot takes off right from there, does a couple of rolls on the climb out, then proceeds to perform a series of fast low dives back and forth in front of the grandstand with rolls, wingover and whipstalls at the tops of the zooms.

The noise is ear-splitting as the plane passes close to the grandstand by less than 100 feet with its fixed-pitch propeller over-revving. Too close! At the top of a zoom to the east, he does a whipstall, and again pushes under and passes the grandstand inverted at no more than 10 feet off the ground. Spectacular! This pilot really knows how to fly, but so low and so close to the grandstand. (Flying was wilder in 1931.)

On the way up in the next zoom to the west, he does a one-and-a-half roll and then another whipstall and again pushes under to pass the grandstand inverted. He levels tangent to the ground, even lower this time! The plane is headed directly toward Jimmy Doolittle and me, sitting there on the edges of our cockpits so that there is no apparent motion from our viewpoint for a few seconds. The situation is imprinted in my memory so deeply, I can still vividly see it in slow motion in detail.

The plane is so close to the ground that I am alarmed that the top of the rudder or fin and the propeller will touch the ground. If the fin touches, the plane is doomed.

I am looking right through the propeller disc at that moment and I can see the pilot hanging out of the cockpit so far that his head is even with the center section of the upper wing! The wings are perfectly level. The propeller kicks up dust as it cuts the tarmac. The top wing touches the tarmac, bounces about a foot and the pilot falls out!

A split second later the wing touches again and the engine digs into the tarmac. Instantly the airplane disintegrates and rolls over and over into a ball of wreckage coming to a stop less than a hundred feet short of crashing into Jimmy's Sirius, and then on into me.

A single rectangular sheet of aluminum—evidently the cowling pan from under the engine mount— rolls edgewise on its four corners and comes to a stop right beside the fuselage of the Sirius. I can actually hear its tinny clatter, for the wreck has stopped and the silence seems stunning before the voices arise from the grandstand in shock. There is no fire. Fortu-

A large airshow crowd mills around, looking over the airplanes including the Pitcairn autogiro in the background.

nately, the big fuel tank was drained.

The well-known, highly skilled and colorful pilot, Speed Holman, one of the founders and chief pilot of Northwest Airlines, is dead. And the show goes on.

It was later determined that the cause of the pilot falling out was the failure of a cracked weld of the fitting on the lower longeron where the seat belt was fastened. It was an old crack as evidenced by the rust.

Shivers ran up my spine when I realized I had thoughtlessly depended on exactly the same type of fitting during my numerous aerobatic exhibitions. Ⓜ

Airshow Accidents

BEGINNING IN THE 1920S, I SAW SEVERAL SERIOUS AND FATAL ACCIDENTS IN PYLON AIR RACES AND FINALLY BECAME OPPOSED TO THEM. SEVERAL GOOD FRIENDS HAD PERISHED. I JUST DON'T SEE MUCH SENSE IN THEM, CONSIDERING THE RISKS INVOLVED.

In 1931, one of my very best friends, Freddie Lund, a superb aerobatic exhibition pilot for Waco, flying a Waco Taperwing, had the tail of his plane cut off by the metal propeller of another participant. He managed to bail out, but he was too low. A sad loss. The other pilot landed his Monocoupe safely.

About 25 or more years ago, after I had been avoiding air races for years, I decided to take my wife Edith to an air race, just to let her see what they are like. It was to be the first annual air show and air race at Cape May, New Jersey. We had a perfect seat in the grandstand.

Six beautifully maintained North American AT-6 airplanes were parked wingtip to wingtip in front of the grandstand. The owner/pilots, their wives and children were busy enthusiastically polishing the planes in anticipation of a scheduled AT-6 pylon air race.

When the time for the air race came, to my dismay they lined up wingtip to wingtip in preparation for a racehorse start. I told Edith I did not like it because of the great danger of that type of start and the even greater danger of all of them rounding the first pylon all at once.

All three pylons were within sight of the grandstand. They took off OK but two of them collided while rounding the first pylon—one crashing and burning, the other returning to land with his canopy wiped off. The other four continued to the second pylon where three of them crashed, two of them burning. The one plane remaining in the air returned to land.

Four fathers were killed in front of their families. It was heartbreaking to see those families sobbing with grief and shock.

Pylon racing is really for making money for the promoters and to thrill a lot of people hoping to see crashes. I tolerate cross-country races, but barely. I am not a competitive pilot.

We can learn the speed of aircraft by scientific testing, safely. I believe that the carnage of pylon air racing has done a lot of harm to aviation. We already know the scientific limits on the speed of propeller-driven aircraft. Racing them around pylons with the danger of high-speed stalls, pilot blackouts and collisions is a dangerous type of ego trip. These are my own opinions, of course, and not necessarily those of anyone else. However, I have observed and participated in a lot of the history of aviation.

In 1932, I was on contract to perform aerobatics at the National Air Races at Cleveland, Ohio, with my Pitcairn autogiro. I was the only pilot who did shows like that with such an aircraft. There were other autogiros there that were flown by the Pitcairn factory pilots and some were owned by corporations for advertising, such as Champion.

Autogiros were the first successful rotary-wing aircraft, before helicopters. Mine was the first one sold to an individual. It was a three-place open cockpit, 330-hp engine and was the latest development in aviation at the time. I knew there would be helicopters later.

There was another pilot, Al Wilson, flying an imitation of one of the earliest types of aircraft, a Curtiss open pusher biplane, representing about the 1913 vintage. He was a superb pilot and had been involved in aviation motion pictures.

Wilson and I were scheduled to fly at the same time—to show the contrast between the oldest and newest types of aircraft. He and I agreed that we would fly in opposite directions in front of the grandstand, apparently on collision courses, very close to each other in passing, and we did so each day of the air show. Then I would do my aerobatics, which included loops—rather spectacular by a rotary-wing aircraft. There had been so much doubt and rumors about the rotors being dangerous that I was determined to prove their strength and safety.

At the end of my aerobatic performance, I would land almost vertically, without roll, in the white circle in front of the grandstand, to show the audience the wonderful ability of the autogiro to make such a landing with the engine stopped. That would convince most skeptics about the safety of the autogiro. Not even the most modern helicopters today can do that safely.

On one of these landings in the circle, I had touched down gently

and just started to pull the rotor brake handle to slow down the rotor when I heard the engine of the pusher right over my head, and then there was a crash. The autogiro shook violently, finally standing up on its nose, the rotor blades striking the ground in front of me.

The pusher biplane had struck the rotor, cut off about five feet of one blade and had then crashed about 100 feet in front of me, killing Al Wilson. I have a 16 mm movie film of the accident that was taken by a man in the grandstand.

What had happened was that Wilson had decided to "buzz" the autogiro, but got caught in the downdraft of air left by the rotor as it descended to the landing. The downdraft pushed him down unexpectedly, and one of his landing wheels struck one of the rotating blades.

The next year, I had another contract to perform at the National Air Races at Los Angeles, at Mines Field (now LAX). In that show I added a roll on top of one of my loops each day. Then I spent about a month giving autogiro instruction to two airplane pilots. That left me only two days to fly all the way to Chicago in my autogiro to appear at the International Air Races—a real task at about 90 mph airspeed!

On the morning I was to start

that long trip, dense fog was right on the ground. There are very high mountains close to Glendale Grand Central Airport (now gone) where I was flying, with the famous Mt. Wilson Astronomical Observatory on top of a 5,000-foot peak just north of the field. No weather reports were available so I called the observatory and they said the observatory was just in the tops of the clouds, with blue sky above.

At that time, airlines had just recently started flying on instruments as a result of Howard Stark's discoveries. Practically no other pilots were proficient at instrument flying. However, I had used Howard's pamphlets to teach myself to fly by the turn indicator, the only gyro instrument in the Pitcairn.

To the surprise of the other pilots on the field, I took off without any radio in the aircraft (there were no radio aids anyway) and made a spiral climb to the 5,000-foot top, thus avoiding the various mountains near the airport. I knew the desert areas to the east and northeast of the mountains would be clear.

My adventures were not over, however. I was flying happily toward Salt Lake City at 10,000 feet in clear smooth air, following pencil lines on the new sectional chart. All of a sudden, there was an extremely violent bump that threw me very

hard against my seat belt, with a very heavy download on the rotor. I had never had such a severe download on a rotor and was frightened that there might be damage to it. It kept right on revolving, but my attention was then changed to a strong gasoline odor that was so dangerous I immediately pulled the mixture control to stop the engine.

I couldn't get to my parachute that was stowed in the front cockpit on top of two old airplane wing tanks holding extra fuel for my long flight to Salt Lake. The tanks were connected to the main fuel tank down in the bottom of the fuselage with temporary tubing and rubber hose.

I looked down ahead of the cockpit flooring and saw the bottom of the fabric-covered fuselage covered in gasoline more than an inch deep, sloshing around. The tanks had been thrown upward and the rubber hose connections had pulled loose, allowing some 25 gallons of fuel to drain into the bottom of the fuselage. I am sure there must have been a static charge on the autogiro that would cause a spark when the metal tailskid touched the ground, but that occurred before the gasoline poured out on it. Lucky me!

I looked around quickly for a Department of Commerce emergency field that I knew should be close to me in the barren desert and finally found it directly under me, for I was right on course. After landing, there was no sign of anything or anyone in sight, other than mesquite bushes shimmering in the heat. The gasoline was draining out of the tailskid area. The temperature was far above 100, without wind.

I calculated that I would have barely enough fuel to get from there to Salt Lake if I ran the engine on very lean mixture. When I was sure that the heat had fully dried the gasoline and the vapor had escaped, I took off and flew to SLC, using lean mixture. The 39-gallon main tank took about 38 gallons. The next day, I made it to Chicago in time for my performance. My bride of two months was waiting for me.

As a contract performer at the 1933 International Air Races at Chicago, my parts on the daily programs were short and simple as usual, so I had time to enjoy the activities. No other pilot was doing such aerobatics with a rotary-wing aircraft until only a few years ago, and that was with one of the military rigid-rotor helicopters.

My autogiro had the usual aerodynamic control surfaces, elevators and rudder and small fixed wings with full span ailerons. The rotor had four blades, 42 feet in diameter. The blades were hinged for flapping and some limited motion edgewise.

I was paid well for my performances so did not participate in races with their extreme risks and unpredictable prize money. Though my aerobatics appeared risky, I proved they were safe by my experience.

One sad event during the races was the fatal crash of one of the best-known female racing pilots, Florence Klingensmith. She was flying a souped-up racer. I was watching her through 12-power binoculars, going by the grandstand at high speed due to a new and more powerful engine.

I could plainly see the concave fabric fairing of the right wing/fuselage area tearing loose and flapping violently in the extra strong slipstream from the propeller, and could even hear its loud flapping noises in the more than 200-mph wind. She quickly closed the throttle, but instead of zooming to get altitude, she continued level and stood up in the cockpit to bail out.

The high wind blew her into a sitting position on the upper side of the rear edge of the cockpit. With the seat-pack parachute hooked solidly under the rear edge of the cockpit, she could not free herself against the strong wind or reach the control stick to fly the airplane. It seemed to fly OK momentarily, but then dived into the ground.

I am sure that if she had zoomed for altitude before trying to bail out she would have found the airplane to be flyable and landable. Or else at a lower air speed she could have successfully climbed out or rolled over and dropped out, if necessary. It is important to plan such quick actions beforehand. So, another fine pilot was sacrificed to pylon racing.

During the unlimited pylon air race, Roscoe Turner, whom I knew well, was flying his very special and very fast racing airplane. In the middle of one of the circuits around the pylons, the engine suddenly failed. However, he had so much speed that he continued around the final pylon and with remarkable skill successfully landed back on the rough sod field with that fast and difficult-to-land racer. Roscoe really knew how to fly.

The participants in the races and air show were invited by Vincent Bendix to attend a dinner and overnight visit at his estate in South Bend, Indiana. All those who flew over were to get free fuel, a welcome gift in those depression days.

Roscoe, due to his engine failure, did not have an airplane to fly and asked me for a ride in my autogiro. He had never flown in one before. Of course, I was happy to take him along with my new bride, Katherine Sague, and some baggage crammed into

Florence Klingensmith

the front open cockpit with them.

During the air races there was another pilot, last name Otto, who had purchased a used PCA-2 autogiro like mine. He had very little experience with the autogiro and flew it in fixed-wing airplane style. He was interested in doing aerobatics with it at air shows, but in my brief conversations with him, I could deduce his lack of experience in aerobatics. He asked me about the airspeeds I used in entries to the loops and also about my birdlike standstill landings—information I considered to be proprietary.

In preparation for the relatively short flight to South Bend, I determined that I had enough fuel to get there and still have room for the free fuel on arrival. I carefully drew pencil lines from the airport north of Chicago down around the south end of Lake Michigan, then on to South Bend, for I did not wish to cross directly across the big lake.

Along the pencil lines, I marked off nine-mile intervals for my expected 90 mph airspeed, six minutes for each nine miles. The weather at Chicago was calm, very hot and humid. When I took off, I watched Otto take off in his autogiro, but he headed east, directly across the lake, evidently planning to beat me to South Bend so he could watch another of my standstill power-off landings.

When I turned around the south end of the lake, there was a little turbulence. Then I noticed that it took more than seven minutes to cover the distance to the next nine-mile marker. So I realized I had encountered an unexpected headwind and would not have enough fuel to get to South Bend safely, if at all.

At that time, there was a Department of Commerce emergency field at McCool, Illinois, west of Gary, Indiana. I landed there and obtained 15 gallons from the emergency supply stored in the beacon tower shack.

It was a very hot and inconvenient job, siphoning it from a drum and then carrying it in a five-gallon can three times to pour it into the autogiro through a chamois skin in a funnel, a slow process in the hot sun. Although I did the work, I think Katherine and Roscoe suffered even more from the sweltering sun and humidity.

When we arrived over South Bend, I looked for the autogiro flown by Otto. It was not there, so I concluded that he had run into that east headwind and had run out of fuel over the lake. Over water he could not determine his decrease in groundspeed.

Sad to say, he had two passengers aboard, one of them being the famous parachute jumper, Spud Manning, who had originated the

Mr. Otto asked me about the airspeeds I used in entries to the loops and also about my birdlike standstill landings—information I considered to be proprietary.

long-delayed free-falls at air shows. I had carried him to 15,000 feet each day at the air races for his jumps, gratis. His girlfriend was with him. Their floating bodies were found a few days later. What if I had changed my mind and followed Otto straight across the lake! Ⓜ

Bootlegger Incident

IN 1932, RIGHT IN THE MIDDLE OF THE GREAT DEPRESSION, I WAS TRYING TO MAKE ENDS MEET BY RUNNING A SOD FIELD AIRPORT AT MY HOMETOWN OF POUGHKEEPSIE, NEW YORK. IT SEEMED NO ONE IN THAT VICINITY COULD AFFORD AN AIRPLANE. THE ONLY TWO LOCAL OWNERS OBVIOUSLY COULD NOT AFFORD THEM FOR THEY NEVER PAID THEIR HANGAR RENT, AND I DID NOT PRESS THEM FOR IT. THEY HAD OX-5 OPEN COCKPIT BIPLANES. CABIN AIRPLANES WERE A RARITY AT THAT TIME.

The bootleggers had to get those airplanes back into the air fast and they paid in cash, real gold-backed dollars in those days, not the scrap paper of today—worth 10 times the latter and practically no income tax!

There was one well-known class of people who could easily afford airplanes to use in their illegal enterprise of bootlegging whiskey over the border from Canada. Those guys were really flush. The New Standard D-25 open cockpit five-place biplane with Wright J-5 225-hp engine was the very best for the job and it was their favorite. It could easily carry a load of 1,000 pounds of bottles of Scotch, packed closely with burlap bags for damage control. One thousand pounds was well over the D-25's normal passenger load of 680 pounds. That airplane was designed specifically for barnstorming in and out of small grass fields, making it ideal for their purpose.

That load of Scotch would often be doubled by the well-organized shops that imported empty bottles from Scotland, diluted the whiskey with prune juice or something and grain alcohol and applied counterfeit labels.

The manufacturer of the D-25 went out of business in 1929 so it was an orphaned airplane, but a very good one. The bootleggers mostly hired unlicensed pilots with limited experience to fly the D-25s. They made from one to three flights a day over the border with loads of good Scotch whiskey which was purchased legally in Canada.

The Canadians were also happily cashing in on our stupid Volstead Act, the origin of our well-known organized crime legacy today.

The planes were landed in various hayfields just south of the border, unloaded into cars by appointment and returned for another load. In the long summer days, they could easily make three round trips a day—and I heard of four.

As they arrived over the designated field, the pilots would look for a whitewashed signal-of-the-day on top of a car before landing, and if any other car was seen in the vicinity, they would go back to Canada without landing and make another appointment. After all, they didn't want to pay off too many revenuers.

Those landings, and some of the pilots who made them, were not always successful, and the airplanes would occasionally get bent out of shape—sometimes a little, sometimes a lot.

It so happened that I had a small business in an 80-by-100-foot hangar where I serviced and rebuilt airplanes. My chief mechanic had been a foreman in the New Standard factory in charge of building the very same D-25s that were being used by the bootleggers and being bent into odd shapes. So it was quite convenient and natural for the airplanes to be brought in trucks to my shop for reshaping. My chief was a real expert, so we had a good business going.

The bootleggers had to get those

airplanes back into the air fast and they paid in cash, real gold-backed dollars in those days, not the scrap paper of today—worth 10 times the latter and practically no income tax! Those bootleggers did not bank their money. They just kept it in big bills in big rolls in their pockets. They didn't want to bother the busy IRS with any extra bookkeeping.

One D-25 arrived by air under its own power but odd looking. The landing gear seemed to be rather spread out and squat looking. Four really big men got out of the front cockpit with their baggage, followed by the pilot and his baggage. It was quite a load. They had flown all the way from Detroit, at least a four-hour flight with a tailwind. They told me their story and it was incredible!

Their pilot had flown a 1,200-pound load of whiskey over the border to a small field at Detroit, but had seen some strange cars near the field. The men in the pickup car waved him off, so he had to return to Canada. However, due to his very light load of fuel, he could not make it, so he elected to land on an exposed sandbar in the center of the river. It was rough and the landing gear spread out due to the fuselage structure parting and the long-erons spreading apart, including the flying wires and the wings!

The border line split the island, but the pilot had landed on the Canadian side of the line. The police came over to the island but they could not touch him as long as he stayed on the Canadian side. So, while they watched, the cargo was unloaded and put into a boat and the pilot took off light. Amazingly, that airplane held together on the 400 nm flight to my airport with that heavy load of meat. A tough airplane.

The D-25 was a plane with aluminum fuselage truss structure and beautiful elliptical wood wings, all covered with fabric. One came in that had burned, all except the tail and the engine with its mount. The wood wing steel fittings, made of welded chrome-molybdenum steel, were salvageable, but we had to build everything else from scratch. Fortunately, we had been building new wood wings, so we had made all the jigs for the numerous sizes of ribs.

Since no new parts were available from the factory, it was necessary to build practically a whole new airplane and attach the original nameplate. I polished the black soot off myself. We fabricated new terneplate fuel tanks and saved the steel landing gear and the aluminum tail that had not been damaged.

Of course, the owner was tearing his hair and gnashing his teeth about the amount of time it was taking and offered us extra money to expedite the job. He was in the hangar talking to me one day, along with another competitor bootlegger who was also waiting for his D-25. Each one had a bodyguard standing there, and each man had two—yes, two—automatic pistols in shoulder holsters. A lot of artillery for protection because they had their pockets full of all that good money.

The bodyguards looked in all directions at all times. I was a little nervous, thinking of what could happen if some other guys came in with Thompson submachine guns, a weapon quite familiar to me since I had used them in the Marine Corps Reserve. Those guys could have them, but the law would not allow me to have one for defense.

A little elderly lady, no more than 100 pounds, entered the hangar from the office and asked if one of us was Mr. Miller. I answered. She looked familiar, but I could not place her. She said she was the head of the local WCTU (Women's Christian Temperance Union). She asked whether I would be willing to make a donation to help retain the Volstead Act from imminent repeal, a campaign promise of the newly elected President Franklin D. Roosevelt. Those two bootleggers could hardly keep from laughing and me, too. I could see it in their eyes and expressions.

I said, "I think we could provide a donation," and I turned to the men and asked, "How about giving this lady a C-note?" They started digging big wads of money out of their pockets and each peeled off a $100 bill and handed it to her.

I cannot describe the expression on that little lady's face when she saw all that money! She stammered some thank-yous as she accepted the two C-notes with trembling hands. She probably had hoped to get a $5 donation at best. I'm certain she had no idea the shop was anything but an ordinary airplane factory and no idea that those men were bootleggers. Of course, the last thing those bootleggers wanted was repeal of the Volstead Act, which was the very foundation of their lucrative business.

The word got around among others who were airplane rebuilding customers, and they all wanted to meet the WCTU lady. In lieu of that, they gave C-notes to me to pass on to the lady when she came back to the shop at regular intervals to dig up more money from her unexpected gold mine.

It was a big joke among the bootlegger crowd, all to no avail. When the Volstead Act was eventually repealed, the bootleggers were out of business—and my shop, too. Broke, I quit the business in 1933, soon after the law was repealed. Ⓜ

Lightning Strikes

IN 1932, I WAS FLYING MY OWN PITCAIRN PCA-2, 330-HP AUTOGIRO IN VERY HAZY, HOT AND HUMID WEATHER FOR MY USUAL AEROBATIC PERFORMANCE AT AN AIRSHOW IN CLARKSBURG, WEST VIRGINIA. SUDDENLY, I REALIZED I WAS HEAD-ON AGAINST A HUGE BLACK THUNDERSTORM. THE VISIBILITY WAS SO SHORT THAT I DID NOT HAVE MUCH WARNING, FOR THE THUNDERSTORM WAS COMING UP RAPIDLY.

After completing the call, I hung up the receiver and stepped back. At that point, with me about three feet from the phone, it exploded with a big flash and a loud bang into dozens of splinters all over the floor.

I retreated a few miles after a 180. An autogiro can be landed in almost any little field and that was the only kind available to me in that rugged area. I picked a small hayfield in a valley across the road from a farmhouse and quickly tied down to the wire fence along the road. I then climbed the fence and ran across the road to the house. The family was ready with the door open for me as I ducked inside with the wind violently blowing dust and pelting me with the first big raindrops at the same time.

I realized that the thunderstorm must have been over the destination airport that was only a few miles ahead. The people there knew that I was coming at about that time, so I decided to call them to let them know I was OK but would be a little late. The phone was the old-fashioned wood box wall-type with a hand crank on the side to initiate the calls. I cranked it and after some effort was able to talk to the airport.

The storm had passed its peak at the airport, they told me, but was at its furious maximum with a heavy cloudburst of rain, high winds, deafening thunder and brilliant flashes at the farmhouse.

After completing the call, I hung up the receiver and stepped back. At that point, with me about three feet from the phone, it exploded with a big flash and a loud bang into dozens of splinters all over the floor. The wires had been hit by lightning and I had just missed being in the midst of the explosion. The farm family and I stood in amazement for a few seconds and then the farmer said, "You aviators sure are hard on telephones!"

One day I was sitting in my autogiro at the Kansas City Airport waiting for my time to fly an exhibition flight. A big black cloud approached from the west but without rain or lightning, so no one in the crowd took cover. Suddenly, a big bolt of lightning struck the point of an umbrella in the center of a round table, killing two men sitting there drinking soft drinks. Fifty or more people who were leaning against the chain link fence were knocked down, some injured.

In thousands of hours of airline flying, I have had a few lightning strikes. It seems that one of the safest places in which to be in a thunderstorm is inside an all-metal airplane. Once when I was a young boy out in a canoe, I saw a lightning strike on the water about 25 yards away. Big bang. Close call!

When there is any hint of possible lightning, take cover quickly —inside. Ⓜ

Close Calls

ONE EVENING IN 1933 I WAS RETURNING FROM A TRIP IN MY D-25 AND FLYING INTO THE OLD VALLEY STREAM, LONG ISLAND AIRPORT. THERE WAS NO RADIO AT THAT TIME, EITHER ON THE GROUND OR IN THE AIRPLANES, SO I DID NOT HAVE ANY INFORMATION ABOUT THE WIND EXCEPT WHAT I COULD JUDGE FROM THE WINDSOCK THAT SHOWED A GOOD STIFF SOUTH SEA BREEZE.

Grumman SF-1 biplane

I entered a left downwind, descending for a south landing, and arrived at about 1,000 feet at midfield and 70 mph IAS. As I started to descend, the airplane suddenly dived. A glance at the airspeed indicator showed about 35 mph. I let the plane dive and opened the throttle wide until enough airspeed was regained, then leveled off with barely safe clearance above ground. To say the least, I was surprised and puzzled.

After landing, I took off again and repeated the downwind descent at a much higher airspeed. Sure enough, there was a very strong warm north land breeze above the strong cooler south sea breeze, with a remarkably smooth line of separation between the two opposite winds. When flying to the north against that strong north wind and descending suddenly into the strong south cool sea-breeze wind, the airspeed of the airplane quickly dropped at least 40 mph.

I learned there had previously been a fatal crash of a Commandair biplane that had suddenly dived into the ground without any apparent reason at the same location.

Then one day in 1935 when I was a member of the Marine Corps Reserve Squadron at Floyd Bennett Field, there was a huge bank of sea fog just offshore, south of the field. We were flying Grumman SF-2 biplanes. I was number three in a formation takeoff to the south, right toward that bank of clouds. The leader misjudged the distance to the bank of clouds and flew right into it.

Number two pilot and I tucked in close to the leader to keep forma-tion in the dense fog. The leader made a beautiful left climbing turn and we followed him through 180 degrees and back out of the fog.

I spoke on the radio to compli-ment him on his great smooth, climbing turn. He said he did not even know he had been turning because his turn indicator—the only instrumentation in the airplane—was dead as a doornail!

He thought he was going to climb out of the top of the fog bank, straight ahead. We had entered the fog at less than 500 feet! Fortunately, he held his climb airspeed, so did not descend into the water. He did not have time to get vertigo with that dead turn indicator faultily assuring him that he was straight ahead.

I had run out of numbers for my close calls, even before that one. Ⓜ

I spoke on the radio to compliment him on his great smooth, climbing turn. He said he did not even know he had been turning because his turn indicator—the only instrumentation in the airplane—was dead as a doornail!

Riding a Wave

I N 1933, I HAD TWO AIRCRAFT BASED AT THE OLD VALLEY STREAM AIRPORT ON LONG ISLAND, NEW YORK. THE ONE INVOLVED IN THIS INTERESTING EVENT WAS A NEW STANDARD D-25, THE SECOND ONE BUILT. IT HAD A 225-HP WRIGHT J-5 ENGINE.

The Darmstadt sailplane, imported from Germany, and crafted entirely of wood veneer, was the forebear of today's wonderful metal sailplanes and the finest and most famous of its day.

PHOTO COURTESY OF NATIONAL SOARING MUSEUM, ELMIRA, NEW YORK

One beautiful calm evening, I was at the field flying the D-25 when a friend of mine—Jack O'Meara, a U.S. Sailplane Champion—asked me to give him a tow so he could take some instrument readings. He wanted me to take him to 1,500 feet and then fly level and straight at just 60 mph IAS. I was happy to do it, and we proceeded on our way. The sun was very low in the west and the air was absolutely smooth—just what he wanted for his tests.

After we were under way, I slowed down to just 60 mph IAS. I soon noticed the plane did not seem to take any more power than it would have without the sailplane. I looked behind me to see if Jack had cut loose. To my surprise, he was flying very close behind me at a steady rate with the 300-foot tow rope looping under and behind him!

I realized he must be riding a wave from the downwash of my bigger and heavier biplane. About halfway out on Long Island, I started the gentlest of all banked turns to the left to bring him back to Valley Stream. I did not want to disturb his wave ride and possibly jerk and break the tow rope. We made it all the way back to Valley Stream, where he cut loose and landed after sunset.

He was delighted with the unusual phenomenon and said that was the experiment he had in mind for several years with the Darmstadt sailplane he had imported from Germany. It was a beautiful aircraft, crafted entirely of wood veneer, the forebear of today's wonderful metal sailplanes and the finest and most famous of its day.

Sadly, Jack was killed in Canada while flight instructing pilots before the U.S. got into World War II.

I became a member of the aviators' fraternity known as the Quiet Birdmen in 1924 before it was fully organized. When I returned to New York after a long absence flying around the U.S. performing at airshows, the Quiet Birdmen had become more organized and had issued membership numbers. I was entitled to a very low number but they were all gone. Jack O'Meara gave me his number with "-A" attached to it—a good favor. I still carry that number and consider it an honor. Ⓜ

Forced Landings

IT WAS A BRIGHT, SUNNY, MILD AND CALM DAY, JANUARY 26, 1934, WHEN I TOOK OFF FROM NEWARK AIRPORT'S GRAVEL SURFACE WITH A HUGE ADVERTISING BANNER TO COVER A SPECIFIED COURSE AROUND NEW YORK CITY.

The 330-hp Wright engine had been overhauled only a few days before and I had full confidence that it would stand up under the hard towing job in the fairly cool air.

The aircraft was a Pitcairn PCA-2 autogiro, the forebear of today's helicopters and ideally suited for the safe towing of banners. It was my own aircraft. I had no insurance.

It was simply not available in those days for that type of flying. Even if it had been, I could not have afforded it in the Great Depression, which was still in full effect.

The method of takeoff to tow a banner with an autogiro at that time was to stretch the banner out on the ground with the last letter upwind and the first letter downwind, then continue downwind with a 400-foot

towing cord that was then attached to the release hook on the tailskid of the autogiro. The takeoff was then made upwind directly over the banner, so that gave 800 feet to get altitude and speed with the autogiro before the banner started peeling off the ground.

This particular banner was the largest I had ever seen towed. It had 37 nine-foot-high letters made of red

I still consider the Pitcairn PCA-2 autogiro as the only inherently safe aircraft ever designed. It had a perfect safety record of no injuries for thousands of hours of flying, much of it by pilots who had no understanding of its aerodynamics or proper flying technique. They crashed almost all of them but walked away without injuries.

cloth. The numerous spreaders were made of bamboo poles. I do not know the banner's weight, but it was plenty heavy. It took at least three men to carry and unroll it.

To this day, I don't know what it advertised. But that was normal because during a busy day of towing several banners in succession, I had all I could do to refuel between tows and study the road maps showing the routes I was to follow. The banners did not belong to me. I was merely towing them on contract by the hour.

The takeoff went quite well in a light north breeze, but the climb was laborious and slow with full power. Flying north, I finally reached 1,200 feet altitude that put me only 1,000 feet above the housetops of North Arlington, New Jersey. I had another 800 feet to go to the specified altitude before turning 180 degrees to fly south along the east edge of the Hudson River to show the banner while circling Manhattan Island.

I was carefully monitoring the engine cylinder head and oil temperatures and considering a slight

When an autogiro engine stops and the autogiro stops dead in the air, everything is silent. My autogiro entered a stable vertical descent at about 1,800 fpm. I heard my loud voice say, "Holy smoke!"

reduction in power to try to get them down a little.

Suddenly, the engine stopped—dead still. So did the airspeed. That banner instantly dragged me to a zero airspeed dead stop in the air. I knew I had no hope for further power, so I pulled the release lever to drop the banner to drape itself over the house-tops of North Arlington. Whatever happened to it, I do not know. I suppose some kids tore it apart.

When an autogiro engine stops and the autogiro stops dead in the air, everything is silent. My autogiro entered a stable vertical descent at about 1,800 fpm. I heard my loud voice say, "Holy smoke!" and instantly I nosed down to gain a little airspeed for control. At the same time, I quickly looked about for some open place to land among all those houses. There was no such space and, by that time, I was down to less than 700 feet above the houses.

Then behind me to the right I saw a cemetery, so I made a 180 to head for it in a steep glide. While doing this, I heard a lot of factory whistles blowing, but I was too busy looking for a spot in the cemetery to realize that they were the customary noon whistles of that era.

Fortunately, autogiros always make autorotative landings and I had become very adept at it. So I was able

to land on a tiny clear area in the cemetery at zero airspeed, with tombstones all around me.

While the rotor was slowing down and I was sitting there in that open cockpit—realizing how lucky I had been to find that little open space—I became conscious of a lot of yelling. There were literally hundreds of school children who had been dismissed for noon lunch. They were pouring into the cemetery and heading for the autogiro. There was a parochial school and another large public school right next to the cemetery fence.

Before I could finish climbing down from the cockpit to the ground, I was surrounded by a mob of kids. The autogiro was then in greater danger from them. I was afraid it would be destroyed by the kids climbing on it.

Then one kid yelled at me to autograph his school notebook and all the rest of them followed. I suddenly remembered the proper procedure in such a case is to yell back at them to form a spiral around the autogiro so that I could write my autograph in turn. A huge spiral of kids soon surrounded me and my precious autogiro while I auto-graphed notebooks until the police arrived and chased them off to their homes for lunch.

Remember how I said, "Holy

smoke"? Well, the landing was made in Holy Cross Cemetery just a few seconds later.

I had to hire off-duty policemen to stand guard over the autogiro until the next morning when a Wright factory mechanic came in the rain to correct the trouble. He found that the valve cams had shifted so as to change the timing just enough to make the engine stop without damage to pistons or valves.

On that Wright R-975-E engine, the valve timing is set by adjusting two serrated discs to mesh, then tightening a bolt that runs through their centers. The overhaul mechanic had gotten the serrations on top of each other instead of meshing properly. When the engine got hot during the long climb, the bolt expanded to let the discs slip just enough to stop the engine.

We pushed the autogiro to a little road trail through the cemetery and, with a little breeze, I took off in about 100 feet.

I was fortunate to be flying an autogiro. An airplane brought to a sudden stop in the air by such a banner would have instantly dived into the ground. But an autogiro is still safe at zero airspeed and a controlled, survivable crash can be made vertically, even if there is not enough altitude to regain a little airspeed to make a normal, gentle landing.

Amelia Earhart crashed into a chainlink fence, then barely cleared over the heads of a crowd of people and crashed, full power, into a group of parked cars, fortunately without occupants. The autogiro and a number of cars were demolished, but no fire occurred. Amelia and her mechanic passenger walked away.

The early autogiros had rotors fixed, both in position and pitch setting. They had no collective or cyclic pitch control as do the helicopters today. Landings were made by making a steep approach at perhaps 30 mph and pulling back on the stick sharply at just the right height so as to make a gently flared landing at practically zero airspeed and zero groundspeed, tailskid first.

Autogiros were always ready for an instant landing. I still consider the Pitcairn PCA-2 as the only inherently safe aircraft ever designed to this day. They had a perfect safety record of no injuries for thousands of hours of flying, much of it by pilots who had no understanding of its aerodynamics or proper flying technique. They crashed almost all of them, but walked away without injury.

One notorious incident was performed by Amelia Earhart. She crashed into a chainlink fence, then barely cleared over the heads of a crowd of people and crashed, full power, into a group of parked cars, fortunately without occupants. The autogiro and a number of cars were demolished, but no fire occurred. Amelia and her mechanic passenger walked away.

Now the only two surviving PCA-2s are in the possession of the Ford Museum and Steven Pitcairn, son of the original manufacturer. The one I owned, S/N 13, was the first purchased by a private individual and first to fly in each direction across the United States. It was also the first rotary-wing aircraft to perform aerobatics that included loops and rolls at airshows.

S/N 13's final days were spent as a crop-duster, but it was destroyed by a hurricane in Florida when its pilot failed to tie down its rotor blades. I had flown it safely, crisscrossing the United States for six years between 1931 and 1936. Ⓜ

Inflight Emergencies

ON A CLEAR NIGHT IN 1934, BEFORE I WAS EMPLOYED BY UNITED AIR LINES, ONE OF THEIR NEW BOEING 247S WAS BLOWN TO PIECES AT 6,000 FEET ALTITUDE SHORTLY SOUTH OF GARY, INDIANA. THERE HAD OBVIOUSLY BEEN A VERY SEVERE EXPLOSION. WITNESSES ON THE GROUND OBSERVED THAT THE AIRPLANE CAME DOWN IN PIECES.

The Boeing 247 was the newest—and by far the most modern—airliner in the world at that time. Analysis of the wreckage showed no signs of explosive residue. So the explosion was not caused by a bomb, but probably by a vapor or explosive gas, most likely gasoline from a tank leakage. The investigation rested, but all tanks in the other airplanes were inspected. It was theorized that an electrical spark from a wire or a static electricity discharge had probably set off the explosion.

A few months later, a baggage door hinge on one of the Boeing airplanes was found to be cracked and two mechanics in the hangar at Midway Airport in Chicago decided to weld it. The welding torch touched off a violent explosion, which killed the two mechanics, destroyed the airplane and damaged the hangar. The tanks in the wings of that airplane had been carefully inspected and there was no evidence of any leaks.

It was finally realized that since the filler necks of the tanks were inside small doors in the upper side of the wings, any fuel that was spilled or overflowed when filling the tanks would flow down inside the wings. The fuel would then flow backward inside to the trailing edge, filling the wings with an explosive mixture of air and gasoline vapor. Fuel then would follow the trailing edge inboard, due to the dihedral angle of the wing, and seep inside the fuselage behind the rear cabin bulkhead. This included the baggage compartment, providing another vapor mixture there.

The solution to the problem was simple. When the airplane was designed, no provision had been made for preventing fuel overflow at the filler neck from dropping down into the wing. Apparently, no one had thought of it. Fuel-tight scuppers with drains were therefore provided around the fuel filler necks with vents and drains for the wings and fuselage. A regulation was adopted requiring all airplanes to be designed in such a way to prevent a repetition of these two disasters.

The early Bonanzas, which had small doors for access to the filler necks, were provided with scuppers around the necks to catch and drain the fuel. The present-day fuel filler caps are flush with the outer surface of the wing and are fuel-tight. But, of course, the wings and fuselage are ventilated and provided with drains.

It seems incredible that such an oversight could have occurred when that fine Boeing airplane was designed. It is also very strange that the investigators did not deduce the cause after the first explosion.

During WWII, I was flying DC-3s, the most modern airliner of the day, for Eastern Air Lines. On one of my scheduled trips from New York to St. Louis, Missouri, I was flying westbound and, after a stop at Louisville, Kentucky, was on the way to Evansville, Indiana, for my next stop. It was a clear summer night. About halfway to Evansville, I suddenly smelled a strong odor of ether. My hair stood on end, even

Boeing 247

where I did not have any hair! My copilot smelled it too and asked me what that stink was.

I reached for the master switch and cut off all electric power in the airplane and told him it was ether and highly explosive. We were then in the dark at 4,000 feet MSL with no lights in or on the airplane, no radio communication or navigation.

The stewardess came forward to the cockpit with a flashlight. I told her to turn off the flashlight and go back and make sure no one was smoking and no one was to light a match or turn on a flashlight. They were to just stay in the pitch dark *on threat of death*!

With the memory of what had happened at Gary and at Midway, I expected the airplane to blow up at any moment. An emergency crash landing could set off an explosion, so I continued on to EVV.

In a DC-3 there is a strong flow of air forward all the way from the rear fuselage area and baggage compartment through the cabin to the cockpit. Opening a side window of the cockpit does not provide ventilation, but it greatly increases the rapidity of that forward airflow from the baggage compartment through the cabin and therefore would increase the vapor. We were already getting woozy from the ether

I suddenly smelled a strong odor of ether. My hair stood on end, even where I did not have any hair! My copilot smelled it too and asked me what that stink was.

57

vapor, so we opened the front air vents to get some fresh air to mix with the vapor so we would not pass out.

I was thinking about the explosion at Gary, expecting at any moment my plane would do the same. I just decided to relax and not think about it, navigate to Evansville and make a good landing in the dark. The landing gear was hydraulically operated, but the landing gear lights were inoperative, so we would just forget the lights and trust the pressure gauge.

I landed south, right past the tower, with no lights or communication, surprising them. At the end of the roll, I opened the doors and ventilated the cabin. It would be too difficult to evacuate the passengers there, because at that time the DC-3 did not have air-stair doors. So I had the plane towed.

It was found there had been an emergency shipment of two five-gallon cans of ether to a hospital in St. Louis. They were rectangular cans with veneer wood sheathing nailed to a wood frame. One nail had worn through the metal can right at the bottom. The vapor pressure of the ether had expelled the entire five gallons into the baggage compartment through that tiny puncture. We off-loaded the full can and proceeded to St. Louis.

I am not sure whether there was any regulation about shipment of such flammable materials in airliners at that time, but I don't think so. There certainly are now! We were fortunate no passengers were smoking.

On another night on that same route, we were over the mountainous area when I suddenly smelled a familiar stink coming from the cabin through the louvers in the door. As before, this stink was unfamiliar to the copilot who asked me about it. The odor was the same I had smelled many times as a farmboy when horses were being fitted with new red-hot iron shoes by a blacksmith. These shoes burned themselves into the protein of the horses' hooves, creating a strong and distinctive odor.

I quickly stepped into the cabin and found the passengers were all asleep. One of them had dropped a lighted cigarette onto a pillow in the next seat. It had burned a hole in the pillowcase and was burning the feathers in the pillow. They, too, are made of protein. I threw the pillow onto the floor and stomped on it to put out the fire. The passenger was irked at me for waking her up. She was in one of the forward seats so the forward flow of air had not taken the odor to the passengers behind her. They were still asleep until the commotion woke them.

EAL had several cabin upholstery fires. One fatal crash happened a few miles north of Florence, South Carolina. The only clues to what happened came by radio messages from the captain. He said a fire had started in the cabin and all of the passengers had been driven forward into the small space of the baggage compartments between the cabin and the cockpit and were even crowded into the cockpit. He was trying to get the plane to Florence but did not make it. The airplane crashed and burned with total fatalities.

Possibly, when the fire burned out through the fuselage skin, the fabric covering of the elevators was burned off. So with the passengers all in the forward location, the forward center of gravity would put the plane into a steep, uncontrollable dive. It is probable the pilots were incapacitated by the smoke. Also, with such a strong nose-heavy condition, if the airplane were slowed down, the elevators would lose their downward force and the plane would dive uncontrollably.

Eastern Air Lines had a very narrow escape from another fire in a DC-3 in the vicinity of Philadelphia, Pennsylvania. One of the passengers decided to place his burning cigarette butt in an in-the-wall type ash holder, the type that pulls out at an angle to accept the butt. However, he unknowingly pulled it too briskly

There was an emergency shipment of two five-gallon cans of ether to a hospital in St. Louis. A nail had worn through the metal can. The vapor pressure of the ether had expelled the entire five gallons into the baggage compartment through that tiny puncture.

and it came out so far that he dropped the burning butt down behind it in the upholstery where it set fire to the heat/noise insulation and the upholstery.

The fire spread quickly. The flight attendant and the male passengers tried to put it out with the extinguisher—along with all the water, milk and coffee available in the galley—without success. The cabin and the cockpit filled with poisonous smoke and everyone on board was severely disabled, including the two pilots. They were on solid instruments but were unable, due to the smoke, to navigate properly to make an instrument approach. The ceiling at PHL was at 200 feet and visibility low.

Finally, in desperation, the captain had to make the decision to descend below the ceiling and take the chance of breaking out without colliding with some building or other obstruction. By the greatest stroke of luck that could possibly occur, the old and closed Camden Airport was directly in front of the airplane and he landed without damage.

Passengers and crew evacuated and were taken to a hospital to recover from smoke inhalation. The fire engines arrived and saved the badly fire-damaged DC-3.

The Camden Airport was small and only a mile from the tall structures in and around Philadelphia.

Passenger cabin of a Douglas DC-3

The huge bridge over the Delaware River was the closest, less than a mile. The pilot made the descent at minimum speed with full flaps, so he was able to land without overshooting the short runway.

On United Air Lines, flying DC-3s at the time, a westbound DC-3 was approaching Cleveland at night, flown by a veteran pilot. A fire broke out in one engine nacelle, so the engine was shut down. The pilot tried to reach CLE and the tower operators saw it burning. It finally dived into the ground with a wing burned off. I don't think the cause of the fire was determined in the investigation at that time.

Years later, an EAL DC-3 had

The fire spread quickly. The flight attendant and the male passengers tried to put it out with the extinguisher—along with all the water, milk and coffee available in the galley—without success.

the same fate in Connecticut. A vacuum pump had failed due to failure of lubrication and generated so much heat it set the plane afire. To prevent repetition, the drive shafts of the pumps were redesigned to shear and stop the rotation of the pump when the torque driving the pump exceeded a certain level, thus stopping the pump. Ⓜ

Early Flying Days

BACK IN 1929 WHEN PITCAIRN HAD A MAIL CONTRACT FROM NEW YORK TO ATLANTA AND LATER ADDED MIAMI TO THE ROUTE, FLYING THE MAIL IN THE OPEN-COCKPIT PITCAIRN MAILWING BIPLANES. MY BARN-STORMING D-25 HAD THE SAME TYPE WRIGHT J-5 ENGINE.

Pitcairn Mailwing biplane

I was making about the same money as air mail pilots but without the risks and problems of night flying and weather—minus the benefit of radio navigation, etc. They had only a turn indicator for what little actual instrument flying they could do, such as getting up above or down through a stratus layer.

The Atlanta field had been the infield of a former horse-racing track, now the great Hartsfield Airport, one of the world's busiest. I remember the hangar on the field had the name BEELER BLEVINS on its roof. I do not know whether it referred to one man or two. I merely remember those big white letters.

Practically all airplanes were still open-cockpit biplanes at that time. Pitcairn Airways became Eastern Air Transport later, forebear of Eastern Air Lines, but only history now.

One night in 1929 when I was flying a D-25 to Atlanta, I approached Richmond Airport, a grass field at that time, and buzzed the hangar to get a look at the lighted windsock. As I banked around the windsock in a fast diving turn, I nearly met another airplane, one of the Mailwings, doing the same thing. It was a big surprise to the other pilot and to me. We met each other in the office after landing. In those days there was practically no such night cross-country flying other than by the air mail airplanes, so he was more surprised than I was.

Later that same night on the way to Atlanta, I ran into a snowstorm after passing Spartanburg, so I turned around and landed there. The field had only a few white boundary lights plus green lights at the ends of the two grass runways. There was no sign of life on the field that late. I taxied the plane directly to the hangar door

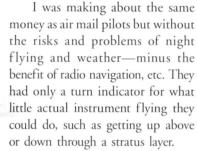

to protect it from a wind that might occur, then thumbed a ride to town.

Early the next morning when I returned to the field, there was a thin coating of dry snow on the ground. Under the engine of the plane I saw a pool of oil that had drained out of the oil tank—all of it! There was also a long trail of oil in the fresh snow, beginning at the point where I had touched down on my landing and continuing to the point where I had parked the plane.

The aluminum elbow—welded to the bottom of the oil tank, taking oil to the pressure pump—had broken off due to engine vibration. I certainly lucked out that night, saved by a snowstorm!

One of the pilots flying that route was Johnny Kytle. On two occasions when he was flying the mail in very low weather—and I mean very bad weather with no radio range to help him navigate—he collided with the rock dome of the 800-foot Stone Mountain. Yes, two different times he lived to tell about it, and without severe injuries.

In the first accident, the plane struck the sloping side of the rock and just stuck there with a broken tree trunk supporting the tail out over the sloping rock. Johnny jumped out of the airplane, not aware in the dark that he was so high above the rock, and broke a leg.

The second time he just grazed the top of the dome and slid to a stop atop the mountain. In the dark he could not safely walk down the steep bare rock, so he waited for daylight. Both airplanes and Johnny were repaired. Johnny was later killed doing some impromptu low aerobatics at Atlanta while off duty. Later, another pilot, I think it was Doug Davis, was killed there in the same way. I wonder whether any other EAL pilot still lives and remembers more details of these events that I have dug out of my memories of 78+ flying years.

Even to the early days of WWII in the 1940s, there was a remarkable sight to be seen in the land areas near Atlanta Airport. At that time the city was very much smaller than it is now, and the area around the airport was still largely farmland. Under just the right conditions—clear weather with the sun just rising or just about to set, the sun's rays almost flat and the hay recently cut—the patterns of the many miles of multiple rows of Civil War trenches could be plainly seen from the air. This was due to the shadows cast by the slight ridges left when the old trenches were filled in.

During the Civil War, Atlanta was besieged for a long time by General Sherman. There were actually hundreds of miles of parallel lines of trenches dug around the city to defend it. There were more offensive trenches outside of the defensive trenches for the siege operation. The trenches were dug with left and right square patterns to prevent enfilading fire along them. (There is a military name, not now remembered by me, for that type of trench layout.) The trenches had long ago been filled in and the land reverted to farming. But there were still little ridges, just enough to cast shadows in the low-angle sunlight to clearly outline the old trenches.

I never did have a camera with me to record that remarkable sight, even when I was flying my regular scheduled trips to Atlanta. The patterns of the trenches were so clearly visible that I could have made very good photos. I often wonder whether any other EAL pilot did get such photos.

Incidentally, Atlanta was one of the earliest airports to have a radio control tower. For many years its chief operator was Ben Faulkner, a brother of Jim Faulkner, one of the Pitcairn factory pilots. Most early towers were on 278 Kc.

At Atlanta in the 1940s, there was a remarkable museum that had a very detailed model of the city during the famous siege. Every detail was depicted, literally many thousands of details, the buildings and houses in various stages of destruction by cannon fire, etc. I have never since seen such a detailed model of anything and I hope to see it again, if it still exists.

Early in WWII an EAL DC-3 was making a very late night instrument approach to ATL in very low weather, said to be a doubtful 200 feet. The airport is at 1,026 feet MSL. At that time we set the altimeters to the height above the field for an approach, not to the height above sea level as at present. Apparently, however, the pilots forgot to set the altimeter to that field level setting, maybe due to fatigue after hours of late night flying from New York.

When they let down to 1,000 feet and thought they were that high above the field, they were actually 26 feet below the field level, over some slightly lower terrain. As the terrain gradually became higher below them, they started to mow down trees and crashed.

All aboard were lost except one in a rear seat: Capt. Eddie Rickenbacker, president of EAL. I visited him in the hospital a few times on my layovers. The above is by my memory of the incident. I never did see the official report.

In about 1929 one of the Pitcairn mail pilots named Banks came to the factory at Pitcairn Field, Willow Grove, Pennsylvania, to pick up a new Mailwing. It was the very first one to have one of the new Wright J6-7 engines of 235 hp instead of the J-5 engine of 225 hp. He made a long shallow test dive across the field. There was a violent shaking of the tail and loud noises were heard on the ground. He throttled back and landed.

The engineers all came out to look at the airplane but could not see anything wrong with it. They claimed they had merely changed to a newer engine, a little lighter.

They asked Banks to repeat the dive so they could see what was happening. Banks said, "OK, it's still your airplane." He repeated the dive across the field and the entire tail came off and fluttered to the ground. The four longerons were twisted off.

Without its tail, the airplane made a high-G half outside half-loop, throwing Banks with the seat still strapped to him out into the air. He got rid of the seat and parachuted safely to the ground.

The half outside loop had reversed the airplane back across the field, gliding on its back without its tail. After a few phugoid oscillations, it passed over the fence at the other side of the field, then under the power and phone wires, accurately squeezing between the two wood poles, and came sliding to a stop on its upper wing in a field on the other side of the road!

Only the legendary Ernst Udet could have deliberately flown through that tight space under those sagging wires. It was brought back to the field on a flatbed truck with little damage beyond loss of its tail. Then the cause of the near disaster was deduced.

The original two elevators were made of welded steel tubing, covered with fabric. They were on one long tube with a single pair of control horns from which control wires went forward to the control stick. However, when the new engine was installed, it was decided to separate the long tube in its center so as to have two identical, interchangeable elevators each with its own control horns. Then the two pairs of control cables were joined about halfway forward to the control stick, with single cables from there forward to the stick.

It had not been foreseen that this arrangement would allow the individual elevators to move up and down opposite to each other. When the dives were made, they did just that, in resonance with each other, and twisted the tail off the airplane.

A similar problem had occurred, without the knowledge of the Pitcairn engineers, in about 1928 at Teterboro Airport during a test flight of a Tri-motor Fokker airliner. However, the tail did not come entirely off the airplane in the air, but dropped off when it was landed. The plane was taxied to the line without a tail, unknown to the pilot until he got out looking for a failed tailskid. The big tail was lying on the ground out on the field!

Due to that narrow escape, special horns with weights were installed on the elevators to balance them. Also, during another test, the ailerons fluttered off the wood wings and the plane was landed safely without them by a very skillful test pilot. The same type of weight-balance horns were installed on the ailerons to solve that problem.

A beautiful little Fokker experimental single-engine, two-seat monoplane shed its ailerons in a fast shallow dive across the airport. The pilot was able to get the plane down with the two ailerons still fluttering down after him. Those were pioneer days!

After EAL bought the DC-2s, Capt. Johnny Gill, one of Eastern's early pilots, took one off at night under a 200-foot ceiling at Richmond. The standard procedure was to switch fuel tanks after getting above 500 feet. As he did so, the valve jammed and both engines stopped. He made a quick, diving 180° turn, broke out of the 200-foot overcast and landed back on the runway. Johnny Gill was a superb pilot.

One day, when he was giving me one of my six-month instrument checkrides, we were out over the middle of New York Harbor when he said, "I'm going to spin it and then you can try it if you like." He entered a spin and instantly recovered by the first turn. It took quite a dive. I will never forget seeing all those ships anchored in the harbor circling around right in front of the nose.

He said to me, "Go ahead and try it, but start to recover instantly when the first turn starts." He told me just how he did it, so I did and it was quite a thrill. I had run spin tests on single-engine airplanes and he knew it. Of course, if there had been a load of passengers back in the cabin, the spin certainly would have been difficult or impossible to stop.

One DC-3 stalled in a thunderstorm in Florida, entered a flat spin and actually crashed into the swamp—and all aboard survived! An airplane in a flat spin acts like an autogiro in vertical descent: The faster it spins, the slower it descends.

I know of a case when a biplane being used for testing Wright engines got into a flat spin. The pilot bailed out. The airplane crashed into a swamp and was not badly damaged, but the pilot drowned when he parachuted into a deep water area and the canopy of the parachute came down on him.

Also, in 1930, an Eaglerock experimental low-wing airplane refused to stop in a flat spin. The pilot was too low to bail out. The airplane, with gear retracted, was hardly damaged and neither was the pilot. But when two other pilots decided to do it unauthorized together deliberately, they were killed. That was the end of a very promising and advanced airplane.

A friend of mine, Benny Jones, spun a New Standard after a 300-hp J-6 engine was installed, heavier than the original J-5. The airplane immediately started a flat spin. He waited too long for bailing out and then had to ride it down, crashing onto a house near Teterboro Airport. He woke up hours later. The extra weight in the nose caused it to rise and flatten the spin. He did not know that extra weight in the nose could cause the same result as if in the tail.

When with EAL in the earlier days, I flew the DC-3 some 5,000 hours and during all of that flying did not have a single engine failure on a scheduled flight, but did have one while on an instrument checkride. A brand-new engine jumped valve timing. They were Wright engines.

The earlier DC-3s had steam-heating systems that gave so much trouble they were replaced by combustion heaters. Otherwise, the airplane

DC-3 refueling

was trouble-free. Many DC-3s still survive and are now being flown by pilots who were not even born when their DC-3s were rolled out of the factory production lines.

I like to wear a belt buckle with a picture of a DC-3 on it, for I flew them more than any other single type. Nearly all of that flying was with the old four-leg low-frequency range stations that provided aural courses.

Nearly all approach minimums were to 200 feet, without glideslopes.

In the mountainous areas, there were often false courses and false cones of silence. There were many tricks of the trade when flying those old ranges. When the static noise level was high, it was very damaging to the pilots' hearing, so most of them had some hearing loss. We did not have headsets with the

new modern circular ear cushions to exclude engine and other outside noises either.

The last time I flew those old four-leg ranges was in 1972 when I flew my own Baron to Alaska where some were still in use. Ⓜ

Early Airline Adventures

I N 1936, I WAS FLYING AS COPILOT FOR UNITED AIR LINES (UAL) AND LEARNING A LOT FROM THE REALLY OLD-TIMER CAPTAINS WHO HAD BEEN FLYING THE POST OFFICE AIR MAIL SERVICE IN THE OLD DH-4 OPEN COCKPIT BIPLANES OF WORLD WAR I VINTAGE WITH LIBERTY 400-HP ENGINES.

The flying in those days was entirely visual, for instrument flying had not been invented. They had flown the mail day and night under incredible weather conditions, and a number of them, about 40, lost their lives.

When National Air Transport (NAT) took over the air mail contract between New York and Chicago, the surviving pilots of the Air Mail Service transferred to NAT. By the time I joined, NAT had combined with Boeing Air Transport to become United Air Lines so I was able to fly the different divisions to Oakland, California. Also, by that time the old-timer pilots had become proficient instrument pilots as a result of Howard Stark teaching the chief pilots how to use the Sperry Turn Indicator.

In 1933, after the artificial horizon and directional gyro had been developed, UAL started flying the first modern airliner, the Boeing 247, replacing the old Ford tri-engine, an all-metal, low-wing twin-engine monoplane with electric retractable landing gear and a tail wheel.

By 1937, the fleet of Boeing 247s had been converted to the Model 247-D with Pratt & Whitney geared radials of 550 hp. They had automatic mixture control and constant-speed propellers, but the propellers would not feather.

These were the first airplanes that were fully de-iced by the same type pneumatic boots still used today. There was alcohol de-icing on the propeller blades, the carburetor air intakes and windshields. The big hemispherical propeller spinner was covered with porous rubber which was soaked with glycerin to prevent icing. This was the first airliner with all these features and equipment.

All the aluminum alloy was gray anodized, such as used on propeller blades today. Control surfaces were fabric covered. No flaps. They carried two pilots, a stewardess, 10 passengers and a lot of cargo. I don't

Boeing 247D—the first modern airliner was a greatly advanced aircraft in its day, but the fuel capacity was too low—approximately 273 gallons.

recall the gross weight, the actual payload or other weights.

The 247-D was a greatly advanced aircraft in its day, but the fuel capacity was too low, approximately 273 gallons. With a cruise speed of about 160 mph at about 80 gph, there was just enough for a little reserve against an average headwind from Newark Airport to Cleveland Airport, about 410 statute miles—not the FAA reserve required today.

This little shortage of fuel caused many adventures. So the company maintained a fueling station at a Department of Commerce emergency field at Kylertown in the coal mining district of central Pennsylvania. This was a grass field with its longest runway lower in the center than the two ends. They had a beautiful double-ended hangar so that two 247-Ds could taxi in, one behind the other and then, after refueling, taxi out the other end.

Refueling was done in the heated hangar from fuel pits and there were heating fans overhead with canvas tubes for pre-heating the engines. There was an office, a shop, radio room space and excellent facilities for the passengers while the planes were being refueled or in case of weather delays. There were no hotels for many miles since the location was really in the outback.

UAL had its own little loop-type radio range station on the field for instrument approaches. Those low frequency range stations were rather tricky in mountainous terrain, which had the effect of causing multiple courses and false "cones of silence," so the pilots had to be very cautious when they used them.

Even at that, approaches were commonly made to 200 feet before glide slopes existed. Approaches at Kylertown were not often made that low due to the station being right on the field, which required circling. Whenever the west wind was strong or the weather was bad, many landings were made at Kylertown. It was an essential field, very essential, especially in winter.

I remember well one night I was in my home near Newark listening on the HF radio to a trip being flown by Capt. Lou Gravis. The weather was very low at Newark when he left, westbound, and closed down behind him. He passed through a cold front and met unforecast strong headwinds.

Due to a prolonged rain, the Kylertown Field was muddy and a landing there was inadvisable due to the probability of getting the plane mired down in the mud. Also, the runway was crosswind and the weather was not at all good. So Lou decided to pass up Kylertown and continue on to Cleveland with a possible landing at Warren, another grass Department of Commerce emergency field.

All the pilots had to know the exact fuel consumption and how to very accurately calculate flight time and fuel remaining at destination. I listened on the HF radio most of the night due to my anxiety about his situation. I heard the conversations between Lou and the dispatchers at Newark and Cleveland, who estimated he would run out of fuel before arriving at CLE.

Lou checked his groundspeed at every radio range station and marker beacon and finally decided that he would pass up Warren and arrive at CLE with four, yes four, gallons of fuel remaining in each tank. The dispatchers wanted him to land at Warren, but he refused due to the deep mud on the field in which another 247-D was already mired. It was a tense drama.

I listened until he got on the ground and got to bed not long before daylight. When he was refueled, it turned out that he was exactly right about the fuel remaining. And I'm sure he was as tense as I was, and I was just listening. Was he rewarded? Yes—with a reprimand.

One night, I was flying as copilot eastbound with Capt. Martin. He was napping while I flew on toward Kylertown and Newark,

The dispatchers wanted Lou to land at Warren, but he refused due to the deep mud on the field in which another 247-D was already mired.

where the weather was getting worse. I decided that a landing at Kylertown would be necessary and I tried not to wake up Martin, making a very gradual descent and approach visually, for I wanted to get a landing there. Very few captains would let the copilots land there as the runway was minimal.

However, when I put the gear down, he woke up and sleepily said, "I have it," right on final final. I could see that he was holding the power on too long and would over-shoot and I said so, but it was too late.

It was in late winter and the sun had come up and melted the surface of the frozen ground enough to make a mud lubricant on top of the ice below the surface of the grass, so there would be nil braking. We normally would land down the slope of the approach end of the runway and roll to a stop on the upslope toward the other end. But we passed completely over the downslope and landed on the upslope toward the end of the runway.

At the end of the runway there were corner markers that consisted of corrugated sheet iron on two-foot steel posts. The left wheel aimed right toward the inner end of one of those markers, and I waited for the noise of the left propeller and wheel hitting it. But there was no sound; we barely missed striking it. We were still

going very fast as we passed the end of the runway and started going downslope in an open field toward a fence and a forest of trees.

Martin had a lot of experience landing airplanes on ice and for fun had learned how to spin them around and then open the throttle to bring the plane to a stop. During the long slide, I was expecting to crash into the trees. He kicked left rudder and right aileron and gave the right engine a full blast of power. The airplane, still sliding smoothly, spun around 180 degrees. As it came around, Martin opened the left engine throttle wide, the airplane came to a full stop and, without hesitation, started back toward the runway. As we passed that steel marker, I looked to see our wheel track right alongside of it with no space between.

We went on back and into the hangar where the ground crew had to wash mud off the entire airplane. They could not understand how it got there. Even the cabin windows were splattered by mud. Surprisingly, the whole performance had been so smooth on that slippery mud that the passengers seemed completely unaware of what had happened.

While refueling and washing was going on, Martin and I walked up in the mud to see the wheel tracks left where they passed the marker and

then spun around. The wheel had just missed the marker with less than an inch to spare and the end of the marker had not been nicked by the propeller. We were moving so rapidly it passed between the blades of the three-blade propeller in perfect synchronization!

Until finally covered by weeds and grass, those prominent tracks were clearly visible to other crews landing at Kylertown for several months, and there was much mystery about who had made them. It remained a secret until I herewith honorably tell about it, since Martin has gone West.

I was at fault for that near disaster by not waking Martin sooner so he could get properly prepared for the landing. He certainly had the skill and presence of mind to prevent it. At that time, we were encouraged to take naps on those long late night flights. Better to be sleeping during cruise than during the landings.

The other narrow escape happened at Kylertown one dark night when I was flying with another captain, whose name I can no longer remember. He was landing on the same runway and just about to touch down on the downslope when I saw a dark line across the runway at the lowest point. That line had never been there before. It was actually a shadow, cast by our own landing

lights that were lower than our eye level since they were on the wings.

I was alarmed and knocked the captain's hands off the throttle levers and pushed them full forward and held them there. We passed over a ditch-like depression right across the runway. The captain took over and landed on the other shorter runway. We walked out to see the ditch and found a depression about three or four feet deep that would surely have thoroughly wrecked the airplane, with the probability of catching fire. It was about 10- to 12-feet wide.

That particular territory is honey-combed by old coal mine tunnels that tend to cave in every now and then. This one had sunk after the last plane had taken off so no one was aware of it. In that area, houses were often tilted and damaged by those cave-ins as the old wood support posts in the tunnels rotted away.

In 1936, there were no regulations regarding instrument flying altitudes and air traffic control. A Scheduled Air Transport Rating was required on the Transport Pilot Certificate. The individual companies (UAL, AAL, TWA) flying west on separate routes out of Newark established their own Inter-Airline Air Traffic Control Agreement, their own minimum cruise altitudes and let-down minimums and approach procedures.

We would copy the company approach procedures from the bulletin board into our own little notebooks for the low frequency four-leg ranges at each airport. Copy machines had not yet been invented. UAL Capt. Jeppesen made up drawings of those approach procedures and sold printed copies to the pilots. And that was the beginning of the present-day Jeppesen Charts.

By agreement, the westbound altitudes were odd thousands and vice versa, just the opposite of what they are today. I remember the night when the Department of Commerce took over the entire air traffic control system established by the airlines.

At 00:01, all altitudes were changed to the present day of even thousands westbound. Before that, the minimum westbound altitude on UAL route to Cleveland was 3,000 feet or approximately 400 feet above the ridges of the Allegheny Mountains. The company minimum for en route terrain clearance was 400 feet on instruments.

So on a westbound flight, for example, after the low-frequency marker beacon at Mercer was identified and passed, a plane could let down to a lower altitude. Then, after passing the marker at Warren, a still lower altitude could be used. Thus, a minimum of 400 feet above terrain could be assured. The lower altitudes were desired to get down below the stronger headwinds, which was necessary due to the limited fuel in the 247-Ds.

Radio navigation was by the low-frequency, four-leg A-N type range stations and low frequency marker beacons. We did not have DF or ADF receivers that early. The range courses were audible and could be heard at low altitudes in hilly terrain because they did not depend on line-of-sight as do the VOR stations today.

The time over a marker beacon was determined by turning the receiver volume down to zero reception when going toward the station, leaving it at that setting. The volume would build up to a maximum as the plane passed over, then fade out again to zero. The time between zero and zero reception, divided by two, subtracted from the clock time when the signal again became audible, would be the actual time over the marker. Then an altitude change would be made.

The low-frequency ranges and markers were sometimes nearly or completely inaudible in precipitation static or lightning static, as were the communication HF frequencies. It was often necessary to turn the volume up high and try to hear the signals or voice through the unbelievable noise of the static. Of course, that was very destructive to our hearing and resulted in severe hearing loss.

In the case of precipitation static, it was possible to slow the airplane down to as low a speed as possible, which would reduce the static enough so that the signals could sometimes be heard briefly.

In 1936 we had the earliest Kollsman sensitive altimeters. One night when I was copilot for still another captain and we were flying westbound to Cleveland, we determined our time over Mercer by the above method in quite noisy precipitation static and on solid instruments in very poor weather. Before starting down to the lower altitude of 400-feet terrain clearance, I first asked for the Cleveland Kollsman altimeter setting. After several repeats, I was able to determine the number.

The captain—an old, crusty and grouchy guy—also heard it and set the Kollsman number, but it was entirely wrong and I said so. He said he knew it was the right number. I had finally heard it clearly and knew that the setting he had used would put us into the terrain below. So I picked up the microphone to ask for a repeat. The captain knocked the microphone out of my hand. He was already starting the descent.

I picked up the microphone and, leaning over toward the right

UAL Capt. Jeppesen made up drawings of those approach procedures and sold printed copies to the pilots. And that was the beginning of the present-day Jeppesen Charts.

window to protect myself, I called for another repeat. This time as we were a little closer to Cleveland, the answer came in clearer and I had been correct. The captain reset to the correct number and never said another word. Another crash avoided! I did not get the CLE landing either.

When flying westbound out of Newark over the 2,600-foot ridges, quite often the static would completely wipe out all radio range reception. Sometimes at night in dense fog or snow, it was not possible to see the glow of the powerful searchlight-type revolving beacons located on the tops of the ridges from our 3,000-foot cruising altitude, 400 feet above them. In that case, by going down to 2,800 feet, it would quite often be possible to see the glow from only 200 feet.

The beacons were about 10 miles apart, but not in perfect alignment with the course for some reason. There were slight changes in the magnetic courses between them and also varying distances. It was necessary to commit to memory all of those numbers, the altitude of each beacon and the Morse code light signals of the course lights on the beacon towers.

To make it possible to see those glows in the fog or snow at night, it was necessary to turn off the instru-

ment panel lights. At that time, the instrument had radiant dial numbers, so it was not difficult to fly on instruments with the lights turned off or in case of an electrical failure.

The radiant dials were deemed illegal due to what I consider the unfounded fear of cancer from the tiny amount of radium mixed with the paint to make it glow. I have spent thousands of hours behind such dials and worn radiant dial wristwatches day and night for 50 years and am still healthy and flying at 97.

One of my flight students in 1930 at Teterboro Airport was a young woman who had worked in a factory painting those dials by hand with a very fine brush. Thousands of times she had "pointed" the brush between her lips to paint those very small numbers. The brush was soaked with the radium-tainted paint. She contracted terminal leukemia and was retired under disability, but she wanted to learn to fly before she died. That case, and others like it in the same factory, led to the law against radiant dials altogether.

Today, that kind of handwork could be replaced by automation, and I think radiant dials should be revived. They are a great safety device in case of electrical failure. For instance, when returning from California in my own plane one night, the instrument light circuit

failed. I was descending through 15,000 feet of very rough clouds, and it would have been a lot more convenient not to have needed to have my wife hold an emergency fluorescent light for me.

By 1936 some major airline airports had acquired paved runways, but runway lights, as we have them today, had not been developed. At Newark, Cleveland and Chicago, for example, there were huge arc lights with Fresnel arc-shaped prism lenses, such as used in marine lighthouses. They were spaced to flood the entire landing area with brilliant light.

To keep from blinding the pilot, a movable shadow bar in front of the lenses was operated by a man who moved the bar to keep its shadow on each plane making a landing. Incidentally, the electricians' unions required the operators to be licensed electricians, a pure featherbed deal, of course.

Cleveland Airport was a huge grass field, but the area in front of the terminal building on the east side of the field was covered by a rectangular area of blacktop, perhaps 2,000 feet or so across. The Boeing 247-Ds could land and take off in any direction on that area without using the grass area.

That black area was flooded with the light at night. If the blacktop surface was wet with rain, it was

sometimes like a black hole unless raindrops were actually splashing down on it to give the pilot the ability to judge the distance above it.

One night in heavy rain I was copilot and the captain was making a landing to the northwest. The floodlight was on my right and behind me. The shadow bar man was accurately keeping the edge of the shadow just barely ahead of the plane on my side. The rain was so heavy that it was impossible to see through the windshield and there were no wipers at that time on any airplanes.

I could plainly see the raindrops splashing into the water in the brilliant light through the RH window, but the captain on the left could not see them due to the shadow of the plane itself. I could see that the captain was not going to level off before hitting hard, still in the glide.

I waited too long before attempting to pull back on the wheel so was too late to avert the terrific blow when we hit bottom. It was almost a crash. I don't think I have ever experienced such a high g landing before then or since.

The magnetic compass was suspended on two small bungee cords—two above and a third below, in the V of the windshield. The bungees actually broke and the compass crashed to the floor, breaking it. While on the ground, the captain did not report it to maintenance, but he took off and flew on instruments to Chicago, using only the directional gyro, set before takeoff to approximate North.

On arrival at Chicago, I stayed at the airport after the captain went home and reported the hard landing to the mechanics. Some landing gear hinge bolts were nearly sheared and some were bent; one wheel was cracked and a tire ruined. They were still inspecting the plane when I left at daylight to get some sleep, so I don't know what else they found, but I have some suspicions.

That black hole at Cleveland was infamous. Today, we have runway lights with which to judge the height above the runway. When I started flying, and until 1930, there was not a single paved runway in the entire United States. The first was built by PAA at Miami.

There was still another black hole—the crew's sleeping quarters in the CLE terminal building that was infested with hungry bedbugs!

Sometimes I think about how we used to fly on instruments across the mountains only 400 feet above them and then cheat sometimes to see the glow of the rotating beacons at only 200 feet.

It is certainly amusing to hear pilots today bragging about

glideslope approaches to 200 feet or even twice that. At Cleveland, the range station was two miles or so to the west of the field, with a big ravine between the range and the field. On more than one occasion, I was copilot with captains who made approaches right to the ground in dense fog. The field was so large that it could not be missed and there were no runways to worry about, so they just let the plane glide with some power until the wheels hit. They knew from experience just how long it took to reach the field and what airspeed and rate of descent to use.

It was done differently at Newark. The field was of black cinders with a swamp between it and the ranger station to the west of the field. The swamp was covered with high cattails and other vegetation. After passing the station, the pilots would let down quickly until they saw the cattails just under the plane, then add power and watch for the edge of that black cinder field to pass under the nose and then chop the power. That was all right in the daytime, but more difficult at night. There had to be just enough visibility close to the ground to be able to see the tops of the weeds.

Today's pilots cannot comprehend how the pilots of those early days flew through thunderstorms when it was usually impossible to

hear the aural radio ranges. So if any attempt was made to sashay around the thunderstorms, it was more than likely that one would just get lost. The obvious solution was to just bore holes in them and hold the heading. The altitudes were from 500 to 4,000 feet. As far as I know, this was done tens of thousands of times without accidents, although there was occasional hail damage.

I learned how to fly through thunderstorms on UAL and later flew DC-3s through hundreds of them as a captain on Eastern Air Lines (EAL). I have flown as copilot on UAL in long series of thunderstorms in those E-W stationary fronts along the course from Newark to Chicago only 400 feet above the ridges of the Alleghenies.

One night we were doing just that in heavy rain and continuous lightning at 3,000 feet (400 feet above the ridges) in a semi-contact condition. Among all the bright lightning flashes, we saw a steady light through the heavy rain on the windshield. It got closer and closer and was bobbing around.

We had heard tales about ball lightning, and at first I thought we were actually seeing one until we realized it was the taillight of another airplane that we were overtaking. We turned to the right barely in time and saw the lights of a slower plane off the left wing as we overtook it.

In those days, absolutely no one was flying instruments other than the airlines, and UAL was the only one on that route. We inquired by radio and on arrival at Cleveland learned that a Pennsylvania National Guard open cockpit airplane was the plane we had seen, and it was then missing. The pilot bailed out shortly after we passed him.

I talked to Col. Victor Dallin, the CO of the guard squadron, and he was glad to hear that the pilot had told the truth about the very bad conditions that caused him to abandon trying to fly that night visually. That pilot's name was Jablonsky.

In the Boeing 247-Ds, it was not uncommon to fly as high as 15,000 or 16,000 feet to keep above icing clouds, especially between Cheyenne, Salt Lake City and Oakland. This was before the development of pressurization. Oxygen systems and masks had not been developed for us at that time.

Over the high terrain between Cheyenne and Salt Lake with nonfeathering propellers, the minimum altitude on instruments was 12,000 feet. If any ice was on the plane, it would be disastrous to have an engine failure. Therefore, it was excusable to stay above the clouds, even though some of the passengers did some "sleeping."

In all the tens of thousands of flights over that route, not one 247-D ever went down due to loss of power. I remember one night landing on that black pad at Cleveland with such a heavy load of ice that cruise power had to be used to land! The ice had come on faster than the boots could break it off.

I left UAL in 1937 to run a test-flight program on the first approved type wingless aircraft, a Kellett KD-1 autogiro, forebearer of the present-day helicopter. After that, I was loaned to Eastern Air Lines to fly it on the first scheduled flight operation in the history of aviation from the roof of a building: the Post Office in the center of Philadelphia. The use of the Kellett autogiro was an experimental one-year air mail contract, carrying the mail to the airport 10 times a day for a year, 1939-1940. The operation was fully successful without accident, even with very adverse wind turbulence on the roof.

I stayed with EAL where I was a captain for 25 years. During WWII, between flights on EAL, I was chief test pilot at Columbia Aircraft Corp. and was testing U.S. Navy aircraft. I retired from EAL after flying DC-2, DC-3, DC-4, DC-7, four types of Lockheed Constellations, the Lockheed L-188 and the DC-8 four-engine jet, in both domestic and oceanic routes. All but the DC-2 and DC-3 were four-engined.

One of the Boeing 247-Ds that I flew on UAL is now hanging prominently in the National Air and Space Museum at Washington, D.C. It is in my logbooks by its numbers. I occasionally fly my Bonanza there to see it.

In July 1998 a British television production company asked me to meet its crew at Paine Field at Everett, Washington, for a program to be made of me and the last Boeing 247-D still flying and now owned by the aviation museum in Seattle. Evidently they scraped the bottom of the barrel and found that I am the only pilot who flew those airplanes on the UAL transcontinental route that is still living and still flying.

A crew of some six or seven people flew in from England via airline with a large load of equipment to shoot the job on July 23. That program is one of the first of a series on classic airliners of the world. I had not flown or seen the Boeing 247-D for 61 years and it was very strange to me. Its controls were so sluggish compared with the modern airplanes of today.

Some pilots I flew with at UAL were WWI-trained and veterans of the really early days of flying the mail. They were a great bunch. Jack Knight was the first to fly the night air mail for the post office from Cheyenne to Chicago in a Liberty-powered DH-4—before radio or even rotating beacons. Jack was the pilot who checked me out for flying the Boeings.

Benny Howard built racing planes on the side. During a transcontinental race, Benny's plane, *Mr. Mulligan*, was forced down by engine failure in the desert. He was trapped in the wreckage and lost a foot as a result. He asked me to fly as his copilot while he took a flight test in a 247-D to prove to the Department of Commerce that he could still fly with an artificial foot. He proved it, but UAL decided it would not be good publicity to have a pilot with only one foot. Benny was manufacturing the civilian Howard DGA-15 that was later used during WWII by the military. He later became a vice president of Douglas.

Walt Addems was check pilot at Chicago, another pilot I very much admired. He was an "early bird" who started to fly before WWI and participated in the first Ford Air Tour in about 1926 flying a Yackey Sport, which was a Thomas Morse Scout changed from a single-place to three-place and from a LeRhone 80-hp rotary to a heavier water-cooled 90-hp Curtiss OX-5.

I believe the first airline to use takeoff and landing checklists in this country was TWA, and Walt Addems got UAL to start using them. He was very insistent about it, with many of the old-timers objecting. But he was an old old-timer, and they had to comply on his checkrides. Ⓜ

Test Pilot Adventures

IN 1931, WITH THE FIRST ROTARY-WING AIRCRAFT ON THE MARKET—THE PITCAIRN PCA-2, A THREE-PLACE, OPEN-COCKPIT AIRCRAFT WITH A 330-HP WRIGHT ENGINE—I MADE THE FIRST TRANSCONTINENTAL FLIGHTS IN EACH DIRECTION WITH SUCH AN AIRCRAFT. IT WAS AN ADVENTURE, BUT NOTHING COMPARED TO THE WONDERFUL FLIGHT BY MY GOOD FRIEND CLYDE PANGBORN. HE REALLY SCORED WITH THE FIRST NONSTOP FLIGHT ACROSS THE PACIFIC!

After my flights, I demonstrated the performance and safety of the autogiro over several of the 48 states at many air shows, including the National Air Races at Cleveland, Los Angeles and the International Air Races at Chicago. That was really test flying, for I looped and rolled on top of loops and many other tough maneuvers to prove the strength of the 42-foot rotor. It consisted of four blades, held outward by centrifugal force and hinged for flapping for supporting the weight of the aircraft plus the forces of such maneuvers.

The shows were convincing, but I never had any competition from other pilots, so was the only one to do so. That autogiro had small wings to take some load off the rotor when in fast forward flight to increase efficiency. There were control surfaces, ailerons, rudder and elevators, just as in fixed-wing airplanes. In more than 2,000 hours of flying, I considered them to be satisfactory.

In 1937, I was flying the first modern airliner, the Boeing 247-D, for UAL, on the transcontinental Main Line route, when the Kellett Autogiro Co. of Philadelphia asked me to take leave to do the testing of their new wingless autogiro (due to my extensive autogiro flying experience). Besides having no wings, it did not have ailerons or elevators. It did have a very small rudder, just for keeping the aircraft headed into the wind, for a rotor does not care in what direction it meets the wind.

The preliminary tests had been conducted by another pilot who had resigned, but Mr. Kellett did not bother to tell me the reason. If he had, I doubt whether I would have taken the job at all. The aircraft had a provisional certificate, pending more testing—another thing that was not explained to me.

At any rate, the tests were long, consisting of many vibration, stability, performance and other tests. These included several flights to Washington, D.C., and to Dayton, Ohio, for Army tests with a cockpit full of recording instrumentation of G-loads, vibrations, stresses on rotor blades, hub and control systems.

When that was finished, I was told I would have to make a dive test. That was the reason for the previous pilot's resignation! Kellett had tried to get other autogiro pilots interested, with no takers. The basic response was, "A dive test with no wings, no elevators and, of all things, only a rotor? No way!" Without knowing about these events, I took the job. As an engineer myself, I just believed in rotary wings and wanted to participate.

By that time, Mr. Kellett and I had flown in the autogiro several times to the old Washington-Hoover Airport (where the Pentagon now stands) to lobby for an air mail contract to operate between the Philadelphia Post Office building in the center of the city and the local airport. The distance was only six miles for a determination of the feasibility of such a radical operation with such a radical aircraft.

While Mr. Kellett lobbied, I carried numerous Post Office officials and members of Congress for rides, landing in parks, streets and the golf course. Most of those who were offered the opportunity were afraid to ride in such a small aircraft, especially one without wings.

The lobbying efforts were successful, so an appropriation for the purpose was made, a bill was passed

When the preliminary tests were finished, I was told I would have to make a dive test. That was the reason for the previous pilot's resignation!

John Miller with Kellet wingless autogiro, 1938

and signed by President Franklin Roosevelt. Of course, such a project would be highly experimental.

Mr. Kellett tried to get several airlines to bid on the contract. All those he contacted turned him down flatly except TWA. But they insisted on a rooftop demonstration at Chicago first.

Against my vigorous protest, Mr. Kellett agreed to it. I warned him that TWA was only interested in getting some publicity from a demonstration of flying from the main post office building to the airport, and they then would lose interest in a one-year contract.

So, I flew the experimental prototype autogiro all the way to Chicago Midway Airport and made two round trips to the roof. I then quickly flew back to Washington to make demonstration flights, picking up mail from E Street and many other hops for the celebration of the 20th anniversary of the start of air mail in 1918. We then learned that TWA had turned down the idea of a mail contract.

There was one major airline that had not yet been contacted by Mr. Kellett, Eastern Air Lines. I asked him to let me do it and I was successful. I was loaned by Kellett to EAL to fly it and made an agreement with EAL that I had the option to stay with them afterward. The contract was for 10 flights a day, six days a week for a year.

No such operation had ever been undertaken and any failure with a crash into surrounding buildings would probably eliminate any in the future. There was no place to land, only to crash! The roof was designed to take such loads, but wind turbulence had not been considered in its design.

When EAL was awarded the contract, they ordered one of the new wingless autogiros, designated the KD-1B. The fully approved Type Certificate was to be awarded after tests of that particular aircraft. To qualify, I had to make the required dive test with the KD-1B before delivery to EAL. The start of the actual rooftop air mail operation was to begin on July 6, 1939.

The aircraft had a lot of special features added for the operation—radio, mail compartment, instrument-flying equipment (instruments), a sliding cockpit canopy, etc. The radio in those days was on HF frequencies and a trailing-wire antenna had to be used and rolled in and out for takeoffs and landings, unlike today with VHF.

The aircraft was finished in time and then I had to make the dive tests. If it failed, the whole plan would be scrapped and the Kellett Co. could go broke!

The aircraft was finished in time and then I had to make the dive tests. If it failed, the whole plan would be scrapped and the Kellett Co. could go broke! The day came and a lot of people were there to see me kill myself!

The day came and a lot of people were there to see me kill myself! Included were Mr. Kellett; several people from the engineering department, including the chief engineer, Richard Prewitt; the Dept. of Commerce inspector, Mr. Bowdwin; and Sid Shannon, vice president/ Operations of EAL—who was not at all in favor of the contract or of the autogiro.

I was briefed on the required dive and pull-out by Prewitt and Bowdwin. I was to make a shallow dive to a certain speed and pull out to a certain G-force. I do not remember the numbers, after 60+ years.

So off I went, to about a 6,000-feet altitude and started the dive. I was watching the airspeed indicator pointer. Shortly before it reached the specified indicated speed, all hell broke loose! That is an entirely insufficient name for it.

I was being thrown around in the cockpit so rapidly and violently that I could not tell what was going on at all. I would see the Delaware River over my head for a fraction of a second, then underneath, then to the side, to the front, all in helter-skelter rapidity. The control stick was out of my hand and was moving so fast that it was invisible, just a blur.

I was being thrown violently against every projection and hard thing in the cockpit. I tried to stand up to bail out, but the centrifugal forces pushed me back into the seat.

I finally decided to try to corral the stick and, if unable to do so, would forcibly crawl out if the altitude got down to 1,000 feet and jump. Even with the prospect of going through the revolving rotor. I was amazingly calm. When all was ready, I quickly clamped my knees and hands together and caught the stick on the first try. Presto! The autogiro instantly calmed down and answered the controls, but still was vibrated from the rotor.

I found the controls operated normally—although the stick was shaking my hand to a blur, but I hung on to it. With the throttle closed, I was in a normal vertical descent and, since everything was under control, I went on down and made a good landing!

The witnesses all said they had heard rapid loud explosive noises while the autogiro was flipping around so rapidly they could not tell what it was doing. They said there was what appeared to be a trail of smoke and fragments of something trailing behind.

The three rotor blades were shattered inward from their tips for about two feet, with only the two-inch steel tube spars showing. All of the plywood covering was missing. While we were talking, thin plywood fragments were still fluttering down.

We found that the 350 pounds of sand that had been in bags in the mail compartment was practically all gone—the bags torn open. They had been thrown around in the compartment so violently that they sprung open the aluminum cover doors, letting the sand out—with the appearance of trailing smoke.

There was no other damage. The rotor hub and the pylon on which it was mounted were OK. The pylon and its aluminum fairing were OK. The rotor blades were not bent. The only damage was the disintegrated and missing plywood covering and the wood ribs at the two outer feet of the blades.

The G-meter showed very high G-loads, but nothing was bent. The

aircraft had been thoroughly tested for strength, no doubt of that! However, due to the wonderful flapping hinges at the roots of the blades, the aircraft had been protected from excess G-loads and stresses. The hinged blades were the invention of Juan de la Cierva, the Spanish inventor of the autogiro.

The inspector, Mr. Bowdwin, said the test was a failure. I gave him an argument and convinced him that any aircraft that went through all that severe abuse and came down under control with so little damage should be awarded its requested ATC approval. I convinced him and he approved it, with a speed limit somewhat below that at which the trouble started. In my numerous previous demonstration flights at many air shows, I had tried to convince the critics of that wonderful safety feature.

In 1939, no engineers in the Western Hemisphere knew anything about what is well known now as Mach 1.0. Over in Germany, without any knowledge of it here in the United States, they already had supersonic wind tunnels and were in the process of designing airplanes to fly approaching closer to Mach 1.0 than any propeller airplane could possibly fly.

The German engineers had discovered the destructive forces and

compressibility of air being penetrated at those high speeds. They were even already designing strongly swept-back wings to get close to Mach 1.0. That was what had destroyed the blade tips, but we merely thought it was due to getting the blade speed too high, not the whole reason. The German research was all kept very secret.

The autogiro blades were replaced and the air mail contract was ready to start. Eastern Air Lines was ready to operate a fully certificated scheduled airline of six miles—the shortest in the world, between Philadelphia across the Delaware River to the airport at Camden. They set up a complete station on the roof of the General Post Office building with radio, teletype, anemometer, etc., the whole works, even a station manager, all as required by the government. They rented a fine hangar for maintenance and had two licensed mechanics, one of them a former mechanic for Pitcairn Autogiro Co., for extra-thorough daily inspection and maintenance, due to the fact that all of the flying was to be right over the densely-built city. Quite a load for a little airline to carry.

When the Congressional bill was written for the authorization and the funds for the operation, I had written into it that the normal weather restrictions for flying were not to apply to the operation of the autogiro, due to its unique flying characteristics. The pilot was to be the only judge of when he would fly, in the weather, etc. That set a precedent which seems to stand today for rotary-wing aircraft, the present-day helicopters.

The roof of the post office building was designed with future helicopters in mind. It was given plenty of strength for the purpose. However, it was a rectangular building, facing north-south with long penthouse structures at least 20 feet high along the east and west sides. The flying area was a channel between them. It had the potential for an aerodynamic disaster with severe turbulence of varying kinds in winds blowing in different directions.

The day before the operation was to start, I carried the well-known band leader, Andre Kostelantez, in the mail compartment to the roof, the first air passenger to be landed on a roof, as far as we could determine.

The airline started operation July 6, 1939, with many prominent people on hand for the ceremony, including, of course, Capt. Eddie Rickenbacker, president of EAL. Bags of air mail "First Day" covers along with the normal air mail filled the mail compartment.

One month after the operation started, World War II started in

John Miller in Kellet autogiro taking off with mail from Philadelphia rooftop in 1939.

Europe, taking the operation off the front pages of the newspapers. So EAL did not get their expected publicity.

I flew the operation for the year's contract—more than 2,500 flights without accident, even with extreme turbulence and winds up to 60 mph. It certainly did prove the zero-speed controllability of the autogiro with its control system using gravity for control by tilting the rotor, as in all helicopters today. In addition, I checked out another pilot as a reserve, John Lukens, who had been a production test pilot at Pitcairn Autogiro Company.

After the operation ended in 1940, I stayed with EAL. Kellett had a twin-rotor helicopter on paper, but I rejected their request to test it because they refused to make a simple change I insisted should be made in the rotor. It killed my successor. My judgment, thanks to my engineering training, saved my life. Ⓜ

The J2F-6 Amphibian (U.S. Navy) manufactured by Columbia Aircraft Corporation of Valley Stream, Long Island, New York, was a redesign of the Grumman J2F-5 but featured a 1,050-hp Wright engine, an upgrade from the previous 700-hp engine.

Amphibian Testing

ALL DURING WWII, I FLEW DC-3S FOR EASTERN AIR LINES BASED IN THE NEW YORK AREA AND FLYING OUT OF NEWARK AND LAGUARDIA. I HAD MOVED MY FAMILY TO A HOME IN LITTLE NECK, LONG ISLAND, TO BE NEAR LAGUARDIA FIELD.

I took on a small contract to make special screws, using my lathe in my home, on my days off from flying. That was for Columbia Aircraft Co. at Valley Stream. Then that company made me their chief engineering test pilot, in addition to flying on the line two days on and two days off.

From then on during the war I was extremely busy. I had been a reserve officer and naval aviator in the U. S. Marine Corps Reserve since 1930, but was a little too old by that time for combat. So I did my duty testing Navy aircraft, some of it quite risky, even though I had a family with three young children.

Columbia had taken on a contract to manufacture a Grumman-designed amphibian, urgently needed by the Navy for air-sea rescue, but Grumman was too busy building fighters to take the contract. The amphibian was a single-engine biplane with a seaplane hull and a landplane fuselage joined together, designated the J2F-5 and named the "Duck." The Navy wanted a more powerful engine to replace the no-longer-available 700-hp engine, and selected a Wright engine of 1,050 hp.

Due to the heavier engine with much more thrust, it was necessary to run detailed engineering tests. Columbia was located on the old Valley Stream Airport, re-opened for the purpose.

When the first prototype amphibian was ready, I started testing it while production started. That began with ordinary stability and stall tests, landing and takeoffs on land and especially on water. Such changes in weight, center-of-gravity location and increase of power and thrust could entail changes in performance, especially in water-flying qualities. No change in location of the step in the bottom of the hull was needed, however, and all went well.

Then there had to be spin tests, with considerable hazard, due to the very unusual slab-sided fuselage and hull configuration and the heavier engine out on the nose. The heavier engine-propeller combination had to be balanced by a lead weight in the tail, and the combination could have disastrous effect on spin recovery.

I did not have any report of the original spin tests at Grumman to go by, so approached this problem very cautiously. I made incipient spin entries in each direction to varying degrees of progression, until finally the airplane snapped into the beginning of the first turn, and then I immediately opposed it.

Finally, I got to a full turn and was able to stop at that exact point as required by the Navy and engineering department. It was required to make three such spins in each direction. I wrote a report on just how to stop the spin before or by the end of the first turn and, thankfully, I was required to go no further.

Next, however, came the reality of testing a seaplane—rough water landings and takeoffs. Waiting for various heights of 2- to 3-foot waves and making repeat tests proved satisfactory.

Finally a day came with the required 4- to 6-foot waves. The temperature of the air was 17 F, well below the freezing temperature of the sea water adjacent to Floyd Bennett Field NAS, where the tests were held. The waves were vicious, but there was a good wind, which would help.

Wet suits had not been developed at that early time so—in spite of the cold—I wore only an ordinary flight suit with an inflatable Mae West life preserver and gloves. No parachute.

There were two Navy rescue boats riding alongside the course of landings and takeoffs, ready to get me out of the water as quickly as possible.

As I taxied down the ramp into the water, a little two-seater Navy SOC center-float seaplane attempted

---

I wrote a report on just how to stop the spin before or by the end of the first turn and, thankfully, I was required to go no further.

The plane plunged through those big violent waves, green water exiting from the cowling behind the air-cooled engine, then slammed down keel first into the next wave with terrifying force, only to dive into another.

to splash down in that extremely rough water instead of seeking a smoother area protected by land. It upset in that extremely rough water and the pilot perished from the cold water before being pulled out. That sad event shook me just before flying out of that same rough water. Consider that those huge four-engine trans-Atlantic flying boats were limited to only 18-inch waves!

I started my takeoff before I lost my nerve. The plane plunged through those big violent waves, green water exiting from the cowling behind the air-cooled engine, then slammed down keel first into the next wave with terrifying force, only to dive into another.

I just held full power and the stick back most of the time until the last wave finally pushed the hull barely over the next one. I held the plane barely above the stall speed over the tops of the waves until I could get speed to climb.

The plane had taken a beating. I looked out on the wings that were covered with salt-water ice from the great splashing and the spray from the propeller. Even my windshield was covered with so much ice I could not see through it.

I considered landing back on the field to have the ice removed before splashing down again, but decided to go ahead and get it over with. We

were running late and if we didn't get the three flights done before sundown, we might not get another day with the required waves.

So down I went between the two rescue boats. The shocks of hitting the waves were extremely jarring, with the water spraying and me praying! Finally the airplane came to a safe stop—pitching and bobbing in the water. I taxied back to the ramp in a strong crosswind and up to have the ice removed.

After that, there were two more successful repeat performances that proved to me that Grumman really knew how to design a fine seaplane. I was already tired and chilled, so if I had been dumped into that cold water, I could not have survived.

Production of the J2F-6 Duck then proceeded at full bore along with the production testing of each plane, several flights each, to get all adjustments and glitches attended to. Several incidents occurred during this phase—some suspected to be caused by deliberate sabotage.

While taxiing out with one plane that had been test-flown about twice before, the plane insisted on turning off one side of the taxiway, and application of rudder made it turn more. I stopped and returned to the ramp.

We found that someone had deliberately crossed the rudder wires!

It took special effort to do so and it could not have been accidental.

Each plane had to be flown to 16,000 feet where fuel flow tests were made from the tanks, and then the engine supercharger blowers had to be shifted into high three times. On one flight, I selected a tank and the engine promptly quit cold and would not come to life at all when the original tank was re-selected.

Since Floyd Bennett NAS was a larger field than Valley Stream and the weather was good, I made a dead-engine landing there. It was found that the one tank was filled with water! That could not have been a mistake. Some people actually liked Hitler!

On another flight, at 16,000 feet, I felt woozy and was talking nonsense to myself. By good fortune, I realized I was hypoxic and looked at the oxygen meter. It was showing zero flow. The valves were set correctly, but no oxygen flowed. I promptly dived down to lower altitude and flew around for a while until I could get some oxygen in my blood before landing. The maintenance department told me the oxygen system had been deliberately disabled by crushing a tube.

The prize-winning event occurred at the same altitude when I shifted the supercharger blower speed. The engine quit to about idling power. Unfortunately, I had climbed up through about a 1,000-foot overcast and had gotten on top at 10,000 feet. I had to make a power-off instrument approach on the old loop-type low-frequency radio range there by means of the A and N signals heard in my headset.

The station was northwest of the field, but approaches were not allowed from that direction because they would be over the densely populated area of Brooklyn. So the approach had to be made from over the ocean toward the station to find the runway before reaching the station. That allowed a plane to be flown down to the lowest approach altitude over the water and some low-lying land to find the runway.

Maybe you can imagine the wild guessing game I had while the amphibian glided like a brick as I made a lot of guesses to get down to land on the runway. If I undershot, I would have water under me, so I kept the hand-operated landing gear retracted.

When I broke out of the 1,000-foot overcast into the dense smog and with a lot of speed, I saw what appeared to be a runway. I had to fly left-handed while I frantically hand-cranked the gear down without being able to look very much outside. I heard the tower call all aircraft to vacate the taxiway, so I

knew that was where I was about to set down. Three airplanes got off the taxiway just in time to let me land. I lucked out that time!

We had to splash down into water with each plane at least once to check for hull leaks, and always tried to do so in fresh water to avoid salt-water contamination of the hull, etc. In the winter it was sometimes difficult to find unfrozen fresh water areas.

On one of these tests in the very cold winter, the only such area I could find was on the Hudson River south of Newburgh, where the fresh water of the river meets the salt sea water tide. One large area looked like it would be fresh water, but it was covered by many broken chunks of ice that would wreck the airplane.

I picked out a clear area and set down between some fairly large icebergs. Immediately after touchdown, the Navy inspector in the rear seat started yelling frantically for me to take off again because we were taking on water. I opened the throttle and picked my way between the chunks of ice toward the south and the saltwater area, but the airplane was so heavy I could not get enough speed to get it up on the step for at least two miles.

I finally did get off, but the airplane was so heavy I had to fly south between the mountains for

miles before I could get enough altitude to turn toward Valley Stream.

I surmised I must have hit a chunk of ice that had gashed the hull. I figured the water would pour out once I got it in the air. However, the airplane did not get any lighter as I struggled for a long time toward Valley Stream with the plane very heavy and sluggish. There also was a tendency to dive or zoom if I did not keep it level, because of the water sloshing fore and aft. When I tried to glide down for the landing, the plane wanted to dive, so I had to raise the nose to shift the water back again into the hull. I then made a level mushing approach to a hard and fast landing.

It was found that there were several drums of water in the hull. It had been forced in under high pressure under the fast-moving hull. There was a large circular V-shaped camera hatch in the keel area of the hull, held down tightly by eight or 10 bolts, but there was no required rubber gasket around the edge of the hatch cover! The water, under high pressure, had been forced inward but then the hatch was forced down by the inside water pressure which prevented it from draining. The Hitler-lovers were at work again, for there had been no reason at all to remove that hatch.

I promptly dived down to lower altitude and flew around for a while until I could get some oxygen in my blood before landing. The maintenance department told me the oxygen system had been deliberately disabled by crushing a tube.

One beautiful warm autumn afternoon with Ted, the Navy inspector, aboard, I flew to Candlewood Lake, a large area of water surrounded by hundreds of summer cottages and boat docks. I splashed down in the center of the lake, far from shore, for the propeller of that airplane made the loudest noise of any aircraft in the service, and I did not wish to disturb the residents too much. While we were floating to check for leaks, we could see no activity whatever along the shores. Residents had apparently gone back home that late in the season.

With no leaks found, we decided to succumb to the desire to dive overboard for a last swim of the season. I shut the engine down, opened the little side door that was about 18 inches above waterline so we could climb back aboard, and we both stripped and dove into the still warm water.

The wind was absolutely calm and the water was as glassy as a mill-pond—not a ripple until we disturbed it. The warm sun was going down and the shadows of the low hills were reaching the shore of the lake.

While we were treading water and talking, I felt a sudden breeze on the back of my wet head. I thought it was from the shadows causing a drop in air temperature and of the ground. But the water was still warm, so convection was beginning. A few minutes later I happened to look back at the airplane and to my surprise, it was rapidly drifting away in that wind, leaving us alone out there in the middle of that big lake. It was headed downwind with its tail into the wind.

I quickly yelled to Ted to stay where he was and I took off swimming to catch the plane. The wind became stronger and the plane went faster. I swam as fast as I could with all of my strength. Just as I was about exhausted, I was finally barely able to grab the wet and slippery rudder. I hung on for a long time while I caught my breath and allowed my pounding heart to slow down. It had been the most desperate exertion of my life.

After I was fairly well rested, but still being dragged farther away from Ted, I had to swim alongside the hull to reach that little door, and then reach up to grab its sill. The plane was going so fast I was barely able to reach the door.

There were no projections on the hull to grab on to for a rest along the way. With all my might, I made one desperate lunge and was able to get my hand over the sill. I hung on for a minute or two while my heart and lungs rested a little, then struggled up into the door. Wet and naked, I climb up into the cockpit.

I have talked to several men who simply worshipped that amphibian because they had been pulled out of the unforgiving ocean into that little door. In exhausted and starved condition, they were put into the folding litters to rest. In some cases, so many men were lifted aboard that the plane could not take off and had to taxi on the water until a surface ship could arrive and take them aboard.

The battery on the Duck was a small one, about the size of a garden tractor battery. It was supposed to start the big engine in an emergency. I could see the sun just about to set and fervently hoped that the engine would start. I carefully primed it and turned the switch. After about two turns, the engine coughed to life with a normal cloud of smoke.

I immediately turned to go back to get Ted as the sun sunk out of sight. I had little hope of finding his small head out in that big lake in the waning light, but about the time I had lost hope, I suddenly saw his arm waving. I taxied alongside him with the engine idling. He was able to grab the sill of the door, but was too weak by that time to pull himself up into the door. With the engine still dragging the plane through the water, I climbed down and dragged him aboard and rushed back up into the cockpit, for I had to fly back to Val-ley Stream as quickly as possible.

Still totally bare, wet and chilled, I took off and headed south, calling on the radio to tell the company tower where I was. That was a cold half-hour ride, even with the cockpit sliding cover closed. There was no heater.

When I landed and the ground crew saw me, stark naked in the cockpit (Ted was clothed by then), there was a lot of hilarity and joking about it. We never heard the end of that incident until the end of the war.

The excellent J2F-6 amphibians played a big part in many rescues during the war, and I am glad I had a part in their production. I have talked to several men who simply worshipped that amphibian because they had been pulled out of the unforgiving ocean into that little door. In exhausted and starved condition, they were put into the folding litters to rest. In some cases, so many men

Foreground: Grumman XJL-1, a monoplane amphibian designed to replace the J2F-6, one of only two built by Columbia Aircraft Corporation.
Background: Grumman J2F-6 "Duck," Columbia built 330 of this type of amphibian. Every amphibian, of both types, were test-piloted by John Miller.

were lifted aboard that the plane could not take off and had to taxi on the water until a surface ship could arrive and take them aboard.

One of my former Marine Corps Reserve squadron pilots, Vern Petersen, now deceased (as a General), made a rescue in a J2F-6 under enemy fire at Guadalcanal, for which I heard he was awarded a medal.

Only four or five of the 330 that were built still exist, one in the EAA Museum at Oshkosh. I tested every one of them. I hope the Navy Museum at Pensacola has one. It deserves a rightful place alongside the fighters there. The San Diego Air and Space Museum had one but, sadly, they sold it.

Now the task of air-sea rescue has been taken over by helicopters.

I had a hand in the early development of rotary-wing aircraft, too, and was awarded an Honorary Fellowship in the Society of Experimental Test Pilots.

During all this testing of the J2F-6 Ducks, there was another amphibian being designed and built, the XJL-1. I was assigned to that. Ⓜ

XJL-1 Amphibian

Early in the production run of the J2F-6 biplane amphibian, the Navy requested that a larger and more modern amphibian be produced for urgent air/sea rescue flying. It happened that Grumman had the preliminary design of such an aircraft on the drawing board, which they turned over to Columbia for finishing and production. This was started and I observed the design work and made some suggestions.

The unusual combination of land-type fuselage and water-type flying boat hull was originated between the wars by Grover Loening, who manufactured his designs for the Army and Navy, such as the OL-8 with modified Liberty engines.

Three airframes were built, one for testing to destruction and the other two for flight. The test airframe was shipped to the government laboratory for test. As the two prototypes progressed, I spent a lot of time in and around them to completely familiarize myself with all of their controls, fuel and electrical systems, landing gear systems, etc. One had a hydraulically operated landing gear and the other a mechanical system of a very unique type—electrically driven screws that had recirculating bearing balls.

These aircraft had nose wheels instead of the old tail wheels as used on previous airplanes, a great safety improvement. The wings, outboard of the landing gear struts, folded upward by actuation systems mentioned above, so that their tips almost touched together over the cockpit canopy to reduce congestion on a flight deck. They had the equipment for catapult launching and an arresting hook.

A fairly large cabin was provided by the hull and there were four fold-down litters on each side-wall for rescued men. On outbound flights, a collapsible neoprene extra fuel bag in the cabin could be filled and it would collapse as the fuel was used. With that outbound fuel, the range was 1,700 nm.

Preparing for a first test flight in newly designed aircraft—especially a complex, complicated type, such as the XJL-1, and a rather radical type at that—requires very careful planning and thorough study of all of its intricate systems, emergency equipment, etc. In the case of this aircraft, it was not only a land plane but also a seaplane, so two separate test flight programs were necessary, each with its own dangers. The seaplane's water performance characteristics can be not only complicated but dangerous if unexpected idiosyncrasies show up.

The unusual combination of land-type fuselage and water-type flying boat hull was originated between the wars by Grover Loening, who manufactured his designs for the Army and Navy, such as the OL-8 with modified Liberty engines. I happened to know Loening, who had been an engineer for the Wright brothers. I visited his factory on the lower east side of Manhattan while I was studying mechanical engineering at Pratt Institute of Technology.

While work was going on in the engineering department and in the manufacturing shop on the airframe parts, a very complicated model test program was being conducted. An exact scale model was built and tested in a wind tunnel to obtain aerodynamic data about performance, etc.

Another exact but larger model was built and powered by electric motors. It was built to actually fly under captive control in the Navy's water testing canal. There was a long canal inside a special test building,

used mainly for testing ship hulls, submarines, torpedoes, etc.

A short traveling bridge rode on rails alongside each side of the canal. A set of controls and a pilot's seat was on the bridge so that a model could be flown via remote mechanical controls, with bridge following. The model actually flies but is held captive within limits. In that way, the water characteristics can be quite well determined in safety before the aircraft is actually built. This can be done with various loads and CG locations

and in artificially induced waves.

I suppose that in these days of electronic radio control, the testing of such a model could be done in actual free-flight under radio control. Such free-flight testing could possibly include spin and dive tests to avoid endangering a pilot in a full-scale aircraft.

Finally, after the first prototype was completed and ready, engine run-up tests were made, and the day came for taxi tests on the ground. They were made at gradually increased speeds and proved satisfac-

tory, including steering control. High-speed runs were made on the 3,000-foot runways, none too long, even with low takeoff weight.

The day finally came for an actual flight after careful check of CG location and engine run-up. An exciting moment! Fire engines and an ambulance were located at the far end of the runway and the first takeoff was made.

The airplane flew beautifully. The landing gear retracted and extended properly and the first landing was normal. The employees

of the factory were outside to see the test flight and they celebrated by cheering and then went back to work. A tense day that ended OK.

The serious work of flight evaluation then began. That started with speed runs while calibrating the air-speed indicator over a measured course out over the water, and watching for signs of control surface flutter at gradually increased speeds (including with the landing gear down). No flutter occurred. All that careful laboratory testing had paid off. There were no problems whatever.

Engine cooling was satisfactory and the propeller worked normally. Numerous tests followed. It was an excellent landplane.

On one of the test flights, I had two engineers riding down in the cabin to take numerous readings of strain gauges on the structures and temperature gauges in the engine area. They were wearing detachable parachute harnesses, but their parachutes were hanging on a side wall ready for use.

Immediately after liftoff, without distance left for an emergency landing straight ahead, an enormous fire erupted from the engine cowling and blew back over the windshield and down into the cockpit on which I had the sliding canopy open for takeoff. I momentarily reduced power and the flames reduced somewhat while I slid the canopy closed to keep the fire out.

The engine seemed to be running OK, so I increased power. I did not wish to crash straight ahead with a burning airplane or to bail out with those two engineers aboard. So I quickly made the decision to use the power to make a power-slipping turn to keep the flames off to the side while I made the tight turn to land on the other runway, which crossed the takeoff runway. I kept the plane turning and slipping almost to the ground, then quickly landed downwind and fast but was able to stop.

I had not tried to activate the fire extinguisher because that would be useless with the engine still under power. After getting on the ground, the fire engine was chasing me down the runway. So I turned to taxi back to meet it, then shut the engine down and flipped the extinguisher switch. Nothing happened!

The firemen squirted foam all over the engine and all was secured. The two engineers exited the plane, choking and gasping from the dense smoke that had filled the cabin. They were scared more than I was, but thankful. I doubt they ever went aloft again.

I have a photo of a large hole failure in the exhaust manifold, which allowed the hot exhaust flames to burn through the multiple pressurized aluminum oil lines used for the experimental readings and caused the intense fire.

That flight confirmed one of the suggestions of changes I had made:

In the cockpit there was a long row of identical switches that controlled numerous items, such as lights, engine cowling, fuel pumps, radios, wing folding, flaps and landing gear operation. Each switch had a tiny identification label, difficult to read—especially in the dark or in rough air. It was necessary to look carefully to identify a switch before acting, to avoid a dangerous mistake.

One of those switches controlled the fire extinguisher for the engine. After I landed I tried to quickly identify the extinguisher switch among that long row of identical levers, but decided to waste no more time and get back to meet the fire engines, post haste.

Later, while I had time to look for the right switch, it took several seconds to identify it, only to find that it didn't work. The reason for that, it was later determined, was that someone had removed the fuse!

I had suggested that such important switches as those for the landing gear and the wing flaps be entirely different from the others and easily identified by feel instead of sight. Those suggestions were deferred until later to be included on production aircraft.

Much later, after the end of the war, when I was checking out another pilot to replace me, he accidentally retracted the landing gear instead of the flaps after rolling almost to a stop after landing. I was sitting in the rear cockpit with no controls, simply talking to him on the interphone. The switches were the cause of this accident that damaged the keel and one wingtip float only slightly. That and the fire were the only damages sustained during the entire test program! The thorough laboratory work certainly paid off.

A series of tests was conducted, too long to describe here, such as speeds and rates of climb at different altitudes, and stall speeds with different weights, with gear extended and retracted, and with different power settings. No problems were encountered.

It was an excellent airplane right from the start, most unusual for a new design. I entered spins and recovered at gradually increased angles of turns until I was sure the plane could be recovered up to one turn. Beyond that, I did not take a chance but left further spin tests until a proper anti-spin chute could be installed, or else for the Navy to conduct them.

Dives were made to a little short of the calculated safe maximum speed, leaving faster dives to the Navy instead of taking a chance on losing an airplane that had cost several million dollars to build. I was falling in love with that plane.

After the tests as a land plane were well along, the tests of the aircraft as a seaplane began. Fast taxiing on the water showed no inclination to porpoise—smooth or choppy water, straight line or curved, fast or slow. It was the best-behaved seaplane I had ever flown, by far.

Finally, the time came to fly off the water, which was done with a light load and a light chop on the surface of Long Island Sound and with Navy speedboats alongside. As a seaplane, it was a dream with all loads and CG locations.

I found that if I adjusted the power, trim and flaps for a speed of 60 knots and rate of descent of 500 fpm, with my hands off the stick, but keeping the airplane flying straight with the turn indicator, by the rudder, I could let it splash down into the water—hands off. The plane would immediately come up on its step and, with my hands still off the stick, I would chop the throttle. It would drop down off of the step and slow down with no porpoising or other bad behavior. This was done with only a light load.

I did not have the opportunity to test that performance with heavier loads, but am confident that it would perform perfectly. After all, such an emergency would likely be with a light fuel load.

One day, I was demonstrating that hands-off splash-down with a Marine Corps officer on board. After the flight, he did not say anything to me. Later, however, I learned he had put me on report with the Marine Corps for reckless flying. I was a Marine Reserve officer and Navy aviator. When news of that report got back to the company, it was quite a joke. The matter did not ever go any further. A Navy officer, naval aviator, when with me on the same type demonstration, was highly complimentary of the aircraft.

That type of approach to a splash-down in the water had wonderful possibilities in military air/sea rescue operations, which often required flying in foggy conditions. It made it possible to get the amphibian down safely in dense fog, glassy water, coal-black darkness or a combination of all three, in a dire emergency.

Rough water tests had to be made to satisfy Navy requirements. Splash-downs and takeoffs had to be demonstrated across five-foot waves. That was the only exciting operation of the entire flight-testing program.

The Navy had some special optical equipment to measure the height of the waves and had rescue speedboats alongside the plane. That was a rough test. The Navy inspectors told me later that some of the waves were a full six feet high. I had green water coming out of the rear of the engine cowling on some of them.

If you think that five-foot waves are not much to cope with, remember that the big four-engine flying boats that used to fly across the Atlantic and Pacific were limited to waves of no more than 18 inches.

If you think that five-foot waves are not much to cope with, remember that the big four-engine flying boats that used to fly across the Atlantic and Pacific were limited to waves of no more than 18 inches.

John Miller at Pima Air Museum, Tucson, Arizona, in 1990 with one of only two XJL-1 amphibians ever built.

Now for the sad part. When the contract was completed, after the end of the war, the two prototype aircraft were delivered to the Navy Test Center at Patuxent, Maryland. After their tests, the airplanes were stripped of engines, etc. and offered for sale as bare airframes. They were bought for a total of only $400 by a test pilot for the Martin Aircraft Co. in Maryland. He intended to re-equip and fly them, but he was killed on a test flight of a large Martin flying boat.

One of the two planes was put back in flying condition with a bigger engine from a B-25. It is now in the Pima Air Museum at Tucson, Arizona. I visited it again in September 2000 when I was flying my Bonanza. The other one is in California where it has been restored and is flown there by its private owner.

If the Navy ever needs a really good and useful amphibian, all they need to do is dig out the blueprints and those two old prototypes. I can just imagine how they would perform with one of the new turbo-prop engines, especially a twin-pack as used in some helicopters. Wow!

It does not seem likely that will ever happen, however, since the new huge helicopters are now king of rescue missions. Ⓜ

I'm sorry, folks, but this was not a movie-style adventurous test-flying story. It was the tamest test flight program I have ever experienced with an absolutely wonderful, docile amphibious aircraft, a proof of wonderful mathematical engineering.

A Challenging Flight

DURING WORLD WAR II, I WAS DOING DOUBLE DUTY, WORKING AS A CAPTAIN ON EASTERN AIR LINES FLYING OUT OF NEWARK AIRPORT AND AS CHIEF TEST PILOT FOR COLUMBIA AIRCRAFT CORP. AT VALLEY STREAM, LONG ISLAND.

On one of the rare days I had at home, I received an urgent call from the airline asking me to rush to Newark for a very special emergency flight. I realized it really must be an emergency all right, since the reason I had the day off from both jobs was that the weather was absolutely stinko with zero/zero fog over the entire eastern half of the United States, bringing the airlines to a standstill.

I drove the 80 miles in that dense fog with real difficulty; it took almost twice as long as the usual trip. I could hardly imagine what was in store for me during those nearly four hours of driving or why they would be calling for me to fly in such weather, especially since there were other pilots living much closer to Newark who were also grounded.

The truth was, I finally found out, no other pilot wanted to fly the trip for several good reasons. First,

the fog was extremely dense right to the ground and expected to be very deep. Second, there was a cargo load of live Bofors antiaircraft ammunition aboard, making the plane about 2,000 pounds overweight. And third, there was no alternate airport other than the destination itself, Atlanta. Although Atlanta also had the same weather, it was expected to open before arrival of the cargo. Dispatch called me, confident that I would cooperate as usual.

Upon my arrival at Newark, I found another captain, Dick Dice, very senior to me, had also volunteered, and I was to be his copilot. Evidently, we were the only two volunteers, and I had done so without knowing about the difficult set of circumstances that confronted us. But I did not renege.

The ammunition was antiaircraft cartridges about 15 inches long. I do not know the caliber. It was for a commonly used Swedish antiair-

craft gun that was urgently needed for a cargo ship due to depart from New Orleans the next day with a load of war materiel. The cartridges were packed, three in each wood box, and loaded all along the floor of the passenger DC-3 and in each passenger seat. Quite a sight!

We were told the CG was OK, but the overload was about 2,000 pounds. I suspected more. It was all more than slightly illegal, but it was wartime and regulations sometimes had to be ignored. (There was probably another thousand pounds worth of regulations being violated, too.)

The fog was so dense we had to be towed out to the runway by one of those special tow tractors made for that purpose. The driver could see better than we could since he was closer to the ground. We could not see the white lines at all over the nose ahead of the windshield with the tailwheel on the ground, or the taxiway and runway markings. After the mechanic driving the tow tractor detached, he pulled the two landing gear safety pins and held them up for both of us to see them.

We ran up the engines and checked the instruments and radios (low-frequency receivers for four-leg

The fog was so dense we had to be towed out to the runway by one of those special tow tractors made for that purpose. The driver could see better than we could since he was closer to the ground.

ranges and HF for communication), set the directional gyro carefully to the runway heading—southwest where there were no high obstructions ahead—and started the long, slow acceleration for takeoff.

It took a long, long time to get the extra airspeed necessary to get airborne with that heavy load aboard, and we did not have any markings to tell us how much runway we had left. We were committed!

An exact heading had to be held to stay on the runway, with occasional glimpses of runway lights in our peripheral vision to assure us. The fog was so dense we could see only a glow from the runway approach lights as we passed over them, since they pointed southwest away from us.

When he was sure he was going to stay in the air without inadvertently touching down, Captain Dice gave me the thumbs-up signal to raise the gear. I already had my left hand on the gear lever. *Surprise*! The gear lever refused to unlock or move at all. All my strength could not move it. Capt. Dice frantically held his thumb up and jabbed it into the air, insistently. But to no avail!

Thoughts raced through my mind that possibly the operator of the tow tractor had played a sabotage trick on us by holding up an extra set of safety pins, leaving the

others in place. We had previously had sabotage attempts by antiSemitic people who were actually pro-Hitler, but they had supposedly been carefully eliminated.

Capt. Dice was having real difficulty getting any climb and was yelling to me about the landing gear above the full takeoff power noise of the engines. He even reached over to try the lever himself. I will not repeat some of the language used in the attempts.

The very slow climb—with the landing gear fully extended—fortunately did get us over the big oil refinery ahead of us at Kearny, New Jersey. But we could actually smell the chemical smoke as we skimmed over it!

The two Wright engines stayed at full takeoff power and were getting hot. Fortunately, with flat terrain ahead we were able to hold level for awhile to get more cooling air before starting a long slow climb to about 1,000 feet. Only a slight reduction of power was possible without losing airspeed and altitude.

So there we were, at low altitude with all kinds of populated areas under us and an overload of ammunition. The engines had to be left in a rich mixture condition to keep them from failing—fuel cooling. There was no choice whatever. We simply had to continue on course,

gain a little altitude and hope the engines would get us to Atlanta. Fat chance!

We did not have autopilots in EAL airplanes (Capt. Eddie's idea), so the hand-flying at that load and low airspeed was tiring. We took turns at it and suspected that the overload was greater than we were told.

We could not imagine what it could be that could prevent the gear from retracting unless a set of safety pins were still in place. But we had plainly seen them in the hands of the tow tractor driver. We conversed with Newark on the radio and even the tow tractor driver came on the radio himself.

I'm sure we must have awakened a lot of people below us that night, including in the city of Washington, D.C. when we passed at 2,000 feet with the poor engines over-revving at almost full takeoff power. We were using fuel at a very high rate, so we were worried about getting to Atlanta anyway. Any attempt to lean the mixture too much caused high oil and cylinder head temperatures. We were busy controlling the engines to prevent failure.

We radioed ahead to Atlanta to prepare to off-load the cargo to another airplane and divide the load between two planes because, even if we did succeed in getting there, the engines in our airplane would have to be changed due to mistreatment. There was no chance whatever of continuing flight if one engine failed. The fuel remaining, if any, was another big IF.

I do not know about Capt. Dice, but I had a sort of calm feeling of resignation to a fiery fate if an engine failed. I really had expectations of it. I thought of my wife and three little children hearing on the morning radio of my fate.

We were a long time getting to the vicinity of Kings Mountain, North Carolina, where a Revolutionary War battle was fought; I usually told my passengers about it over the P/A system. I was thinking about that while we were still on instruments and Atlanta still below minimums, when the left engine suddenly started to vibrate, shaking the entire airplane.

The oil pressure was OK and strangely enough was staying at redline temp. Fortunately, the engine kept right on running with that steady sharp vibration. Switching the ignition had no effect, so I concluded that both spark plugs had failed on one cylinder.

We had not tried the ignition before because of the high power, so we had no warning of one spark plug failing. I was rushing ideas through my mind and suspected some metal was flying around in the dead cylinder that would batter the spark plugs.

Because the fast fuel burnoff had lightened the airplane, the loss of power was not serious. But total failure of the engine would mean a dead-engine crash in that rolling farm country in a dark night. We were mighty scared.

I intermittently tried the landing control lever without success, pondering why it would not release and operate. In reviewing the landing locking system in my mind, it suddenly dawned on me that there was an uplock cable that was extra taut due to the deflection of the wings under their unusually heavy overload. I tried the gear lever again, but it was still locked.

I was flying at that moment, so I quickly shoved the wheel forward sharply to momentarily unload the wings. At the same time, with my left hand on the gear lever, it unlocked and came up to the retract position and the gear came up while Capt. Dice was trying instinctively to overcome my sudden push on the wheel. Before pushing forward, I had slowly raised the nose a little. What a relief!

With the engine about to fail, we were able to reduce power and continue on to Atlanta, which had suddenly opened up wide due to a warm front passage. The engine kept right on running with its steady vibration as we taxied to the hangar.

When we stopped the engines, a column of oil smoke arose from the cowling of the left engine and a small stream of oil ran down to the tarmac. The mechanics removed the cowling and—not to our surprise—the master cylinder No.1 had a big open crack right across its head.

It was after midnight but I stayed at the airport instead of going to the hotel because I wanted to see what had caused the trouble. The mechanics were curious, too. They removed the cylinder and found the reason: The top of the piston had been pounded thousands of times by a piece of metal and had been distorted to a concave surface without being punctured. The head of the exhaust valve was missing, with only the broken valve stem showing. It had done all of that pounding and had finally escaped through the exhaust port into the exhaust pipe. The tapered end section of the pipe had a long slot for the exhaust gases but too narrow for the valve head to escape through it.

The section was removed and there was the head of the exhaust valve, neatly folded double! While it was at red heat and had broken off of its stem, it had been quickly folded tightly double while hot and soft by the piston crushing it edgewise.

By the greatest good fortune for

I do not know about Capt. Dice, but I had a sort of calm feeling of resignation to a fiery fate if an engine failed. I really had expectations of it.

us, it had not punctured the piston, which would certainly have caused a fully catastrophic failure of the engine. Since Dick Dice had priority as captain, he was entitled to keep the valve. As for the failure of the landing gear to retract, I wonder why I had not thought of that sooner.

John Miller with two planes he has flown: EAL DC-3 #344 and UAL Boeing NC13369 (in lower background)

As Bonanza pilots know, it is a *faux pas* to crank up the landing gear by hand. Such stress on the gearing may cause a failure in the gearbox. The failure might not happen at the time of the cranking but possibly later at an inconvenient time.

When I was flying the DC-8 out of JFK, I sometimes landed late at night just barely ahead of the sea fog rolling in off the Atlantic that covered the airport with dense fog. It could happen with only a few minutes warning, and one night that's just what happened.

When I finished the debriefing in the operations office, the airport was covered by dense sea fog. My trusty little Model C Bonanza was sitting out there in it and I wanted to get home, as usual. The weather at POU (Dutchess County Airport at Poughkeepsie) was showing 900/2 and expected to go down to below 500/1 later. The legal minimum on the only VOR approach was 600 feet. Syracuse was my alternate, quite a long way but well within my range, and with Buffalo open.

I was driven out to my very damp steed. The tower operator recognized my voice and said, "Any runway you wish, captain." I chose Runway 4. I was the only airline pilot in the entire New York area who regularly commuted to my flights by private airplane, so the control tower operators knew me well.

Knowing that the top would be about 1,000 feet, I took off in the dense fog. In the climb, I flipped the landing gear switch to retract. But it didn't! Two or three trials, the same result. The circuit breaker was still engaged and pressing it gave no help either.

By that time I was on top, temporarily, for I had a low overcast ahead of me at POU. If the weather went below minimums, I could not land because the MDA was the definite limit. No landing could be made with runway in sight only at that time. In case I had to go to my alternate, SYR, with the gear down all of the way, I could run low on fuel. So I wanted to get the gear up.

I remembered how I had unloaded the wings in the DC-3 (a long time before jet airliners), so I made a series of short zooms and short pushovers. Each time I got a few turns of the crank while the weight of the landing gear was zero and there was no load on the gears in the box, and presto! The gear was safely up.

The weather at POU stayed above minimums, and I got home on schedule. The gear switch had failed, but it worked OK for extension. Ⓜ

Little Thing Equals Big Trouble

I DO NOT NOW REMEMBER THE NAMES OF THE CONSTELLATION CREW INVOLVED IN THIS UNUSUAL INCIDENT, BUT AM FAMILIAR WITH WHAT HAPPENED. THE CONSTELLATION WAS FLYING OVER CENTRAL MARYLAND AND DEVIATING AROUND A HEAVY THUNDERSTORM WHEN SOME HAIL WAS ENCOUNTERED BRIEFLY.

The entire airplane instantly started a violent shuddering, so severe that the ceiling panels started falling and the baggage was being ejected from the overhead bins and falling on the passengers, including the EAL chief of maintenance who happened to be in a rearmost seat.

The rear portion of the fuselage was being twisted violently and the airplane was in extreme danger of fatal damage. The crew was helpless, but reduced power even more than before when the moderate turbulence required it, and started a slow descent while trying to retain control.

The maintenance chief tried to walk forward to be of help to the crew but was unable to do so on his feet. So he crawled all the way forward to the flight deck. He strongly agreed with the crew that an immediate belly landing in the flat terrain below was imperative. The passengers and flight attendants were

terrified as well as the crew, because the shaking was so violent.

Quite a long distance before the touchdown point, a wood power line pole was struck by one wing, opening a gash and allowing a stream of gasoline to trail behind the airplane in the grass. The fuel was ignited, evidently by sparks from the wires, and the flames were traveling along following the airplane. It was quite a long distance to eventually catch up with the airplane, which was lying on the ground with fuel spilling.

The landing was made successfully without severe damage, and I believe no one aboard was injured seriously by the landing itself. There were some minor injuries, however, due to the falling ceiling panels and baggage.

The flight engineer, who told me this story, exited the airplane out on a wing and saw the flame traveling toward the airplane. While the passengers were exiting, he re-entered the cockpit for a fire extinguisher, went out and slid off the trailing edge of the wing, then ran

Quite a long distance from the touchdown point, a wood power line pole was struck by one wing, opening a gash and allowing a stream of gasoline to trail behind the airplane in the grass. The fuel was ignited, evidently by sparks from the wires, and the flames were traveling along following the airplane.

back and put out the fire before it reached the airplane. That was very fortunate. If he had not been able to do it in time, there surely would have been a serious fire and probably fatalities.

The cause of such extremely violent gyrations of the airplane was a complete mystery. It was obviously connected to the hail, since it began just as the hail struck. The airplane was loaded on a barge and transported through lakes and canals to the inland waterway and finally all the way to Miami International Airport for repairs at the maintenance base, a fortunate convenience.

The airplane had major damage due to the violent twisting of the tri-tail. There was great wrinkling of the fuselage skin forward of the tail area for some distance ahead. There was no indication of damage to the tail itself that would cause it to shake so violently. On test flights, the airplane behaved perfectly, so the cause of the trouble was unknown.

The FAA inspectors and engineers of EAL and Lockheed questioned the crew thoroughly and repeatedly, trying to find some item that might have been involved. No one had a clue, until finally the flight engineer faintly remembered seeing one little seemingly inconsequential item, the only one uncovered by the questioning.

When he had climbed out on the wing, he noticed that a small access door on the hump of the camber behind the leading edge of the wing was unlatched and open. He remembered it because at the time he also remembered that he had definitely checked it for being closed and latched before departure. In the excitement after the crash, he had assumed that the severe vibration of the airplane had unlatched it.

This little access door was no larger that six inches square and was for a filler neck of a reservoir of hydraulic fluid. It was hinged at its forward edge and latched at its trailing edge by a latch mechanism about 1" x 2", called a Hartwell latch. The latch release button was only about 3/4-inch diameter!

It was decided that perhaps a hailstone had hit that button and allowed the door to trail in the airstream, partly open. Since the partly open door was so small and located so far ahead of the tail, 50 or more feet, it seemed like it could not be the culprit. However, it was decided to remove the latch and rig up a cable system between the door and the cockpit, so that the door could be held either closed or allowed to trail while in flight.

On a test flight, every time the tension on the cable was released, the door would open an inch or two and

EAL Capt. John Miller with copilot "Tack" Marshall in front of the Super Constellation they flew.

the severe tail twisting recurred. Eureka!

Here is what was happening, or what engineers deduced: When the door was unlatched by a hailstone striking the release button, the great difference in air pressure between the inside of the wing and the low pressure of the high speed air over the camber of the wing caused the door to open and trail. That released low-speed air from the inside of the wing to flow out of the small opening, underneath the very high-speed air.

The extreme difference in the speeds of the exiting air and the outside air caused a series of violently spinning rolls of air (vortices) to travel all the way back past the stabilizer to the elevator on that side. The rolls of air on the elevator shook

it up and down. That caused a resonance between the elevators on the opposite sides of the stabilizer.

It happened that the frequency of the air rolls striking the elevator was near the resonance frequency of the elevators. Hence there was a build-up of severe oscillation of the elevators opposite to each other, causing violent twisting of the tail end of the fuselage.

There was no doubt whatever among the crew that a continuation of the condition would have caused a complete loss of the tail. This opinion was also held by the engineers, including I believe, a Lockheed engineer. They were extremely fortunate to get the airplane down on the ground in time.

I assume that the Hartwell

fastener was replaced by a good ole Dzus fastener. Mr. Dzus was still alive at that time and died only a few years ago. It is interesting that the Hartwell type latch, which is a very good one, was invented in Germany during WWII and was first found on a late model ME-209 shot down in Africa.

I have four of these latches on my 56TC Baron for the two oil filler doors. The factory installed only one on each door, but the doors were bulging outward excessively in flight due to the pressure inside the engine cowling. So I made two new doors and installed two Hartwells on each door. Being parallel to the air stream, they will not be struck by hail. Think of all of the Constellations that had even more severe hail damage, and yet this release

button had not been struck before.

Bonanza pilots who have had a cabin door open in flight may have noticed the tail-buffeting that occurs, especially as the plane is starting to level off for the landing. I had that occur twice with a Model C Bonanza before installing a newer latching system on the door. In each case, I landed with full normal flaps.

I do not know how it would be with half flaps or with none. At any rate, little things can have big unhappy results in aerodynamics!

Ⓜ

93

Bird Strike!

BACK IN THE 1950S, BEFORE I WAS FLYING THE FOUR-JET POWERED DC-8, I WAS FLYING FOR EASTERN AIR LINES ON A SCHEDULE BETWEEN NEW YORK AND SAN ANTONIO, TEXAS, USING DC-7S AND THE SUPER-G CONSTELLATIONS ALTERNATIVELY (A PRACTICE LATER DISCONTINUED). THOSE AIRLINERS USED THE MOST MODERN PISTON ENGINES OF THE DAY, FOUR ON EACH AIRPLANE, THE REMARKABLE 3300-HP WRIGHT 3350 COMPOUND, WITH A TBO OF 3700 HOURS. THE AIRPLANES CRUISED AT ABOUT 350 MPH.

The tremendous kinetic energy of the mass of the goose had penetrated both the rubber boot and the thick aluminum with ease, leaving a huge jagged hole about a foot wide and two feet long.

One day I took off from Houston, Texas, eastbound for a nonstop flight to JFK in one of the DC-7s. The airplane was fully loaded with fuel and passengers. The weather was good but extremely hazy, with visibility maybe two miles under the ceiling of just over 2,000 feet where we were held by ATC due to westbound traffic above us at 3,000.

I had planned to fly at 21,000 feet and was talking to the controller while the copilot was flying. We were moving at about 300 knots just under the ceiling waiting for clearance to climb, when we both saw a formation of Canada geese ahead, right at our altitude.

With only a fraction of a second to react, the copilot raised the right wing to miss them but then said, "We hit one, there's a hole in the wing." I had not felt any shock or heard the strike. I moved out of my seat to get over to the right side of the big, wide cockpit to look back at the wing and saw a large hole in the metal leading edge.

The airplane was flying normally, but we had to turn around to land at Houston. I decided to land with the fuel overweight because I did not wish to dump hundreds of gallons of leaded gasoline over the countryside and populated areas from that low altitude, or even go out over the Gulf of Mexico to do so.

The airplane would have to be ferried to Miami for repair and therefore an overweight inspection would not have to be performed for such a nonrevenue flight. The landing was made uneventfully, for the airplane flew normally right to the ground. I made sure to make a very gentle and smooth landing with all of that heavy fuel out in the wings. The passengers actually applauded the smooth landing, just like in a theater! They did not know that I cheated by gently touching down first on the left and then on the right wheels, with a slight bank to the left—an old trick.

Delta Airlines, our devoted competitor, got our load of cargo and passengers to fly to New York. I was then assigned to fly the airplane to the EAL maintenance base at Miami for repairs, then deadhead to New York for a very late arrival home.

I climbed a tall stepladder to extract the dead goose from the enormous hole in the wing. The hole was located just outside the slipstream of the RH propeller. The tremendous kinetic energy of the mass of the goose had penetrated the thick aluminum with ease, leaving a huge jagged hole about a foot wide and two feet long. A cannonball could not have done it any better.

For the flight to MIA, the mechanics offered to put a temporary patch over the hole with sheet aluminum held by sheet-metal screws. But that would delay the trip to MIA by at least three hours. Then I would not get back to New York until long after midnight, probably 2 a.m., or even later. With still a 92-mile drive to my home at Poughkeepsie, I turned down their offer. I told them the airplane flew normally and it would not be necessary.

We took off for a direct flight across part of the Gulf of Mexico. Minus passengers and cargo, the plane had a big reduction in weight.

After we gained a little speed for the climb—with most of the runway behind us—a terrific shaking of the airplane began that scared the daylights out of me, my copilot and flight engineer. I reduced power as much as I could to limit speed in the climb to about 500 feet, then started a careful turn to return to the runway.

The wings were rocking left and right rapidly with the control wheel oscillating in spite of my efforts to steady it. The outboard engines were being shaken up and down violently, so much so that I feared they might be thrown off.

I could see waves appearing and disappearing alternately in the skins of the nacelles as they were bent up and down. The vertical motion of the outboard engines and nacelles was of truly startling amplitude, about two feet at the propeller hubs, it seemed. I really expected one or both engines would be shaken off at any moment.

At minimum power and speed, I made a gentle turn and got back to make a downwind landing. It was a normal one, for the shaking stopped just as I slowed down to make the actual landing. Witnesses on the ground, including the control tower operators, said they noticed the wings seemed to flutter during the departure and the approach.

The mechanics examined the plane and found some permanent wrinkles in the skins of the nacelles but no further damage. They then covered the hole as they had previously offered to do, and I flew the airplane directly to Miami. I managed to arrive home in Poughkeepsie at about sunrise—very sleepy.

Now, what caused this totally unexpected and spectacular performance? After it was over, my engineering training helped me deduce the cause. When the first takeoff was made with the full load, the wings were under maximum normal stress. Therefore, under that tension they had a certain frequency, similar to a violin string, a high frequency due to the high tension under heavy load and bending.

However, when the takeoff was made with the lighter load, the wings had a far lower stress and therefore a much lower frequency. When the turbulent air from that big hole flowed up over the camber of the wing and reached the inner end of the right aileron, it caused the aileron to flutter at the natural frequency "period" of the aileron control system and wings.

The RH ailerons would move up and down due to the air turbulence from the hole. The LH aileron would move in the opposite direction, with the control wheel oscillating rapidly in sequence, thus shaking the wings.

The "period" of the aileron system happened to be close to that of the nacelles, causing them to shake up and down violently as the energy built up to a dangerous degree. This transferred energy back and forth between the aileron/wing combination and the nacelles, trying to shake them off.

It was indeed fortunate that the critical combination of natural frequencies didn't occur in the air when the goose first struck. The much higher energy level might have caused a disaster.

Except for one with a DC-3, I had already had some bird strikes without damage. Approaching Washington National Airport from the south and at a low altitude for approach to runway 36, a pelican was hit by the right wing in just about

A terrific shaking of the airplane began that scared the daylights out of me, my copilot and flight engineer.

HE HOUSTON

World-Wide Service of Associated Press. United Press: Houston's

ON 1, TEXAS, WEDNESDAY, JULY 10, 1957   TELEPHONE

A MIGHTY OLD BIRD IS THE...

A high flying pelican, remnants of which are being removed by Flight Capt John M. Miller of Poughkeepsie, NY, caused this damage to the wing of an Eastern Air Lines plane en route to New York from Houston with 68 passengers aboard Tuesday. The plane hit the big beaked bird while flying through a flock of about 20 birds about 9:30 AM near Baytown. It caused an estimated $10,000 damage and Capt Miller turned back to Houston International Airport. At right is Flight Engineer Bob Massie, Plainfield, NY.—Post Photo by Owen Johnson

Photos of John pulling the goose out of the large hole in the wing of a DC-8
were published in newspapers all over the country.

the same location as in the case of the DC-7 years later. A large dent in the leading edge did not have any noticeable effect, so I continued on to LGA at New York.

On a night flight in my Bell 47 helicopter, I apparently flew through a flock of migrating geese. One penetrated the plexiglass bubble, shattering a large hole in it. Fortunately, it hit right in front of the control pedestal so it did not hit me. The remains proved to be a Canada goose. (I took it home and ate it.)

I did not know at that time that these geese prefer to do their migration flying at night. It happened right over the center of a wide part of the Hudson River in a very black night. I have since been advised that the geese are known to follow the Hudson River when migrating, so I suppose they would also follow other north-south rivers too. No one would ever have found the wreckage or me, for no flight plan was filed.

Incidentally, in both cases of the bird strikes on the DC-3 and DC-7, the landing lights were on. It is well known that some night-migrating birds are attracted to lights. The lights on the tall buildings in New York City are often turned off in migration seasons to prevent the deaths of hundreds of birds that are attracted to the lights and are killed by striking them at high flying speeds, falling to the streets below.

I even have some doubts about the advisability of using landing lights during departures and approaches in daytime, so I don't, unless the tower asks.

Now for a real puzzle. One of the EAL Lockheed Electra four-engine turboprop airliners was flying eastbound between San Antonio and Houston late at night and between layers at 21,000 feet. It struck a duck squarely with the radome nose. The duck penetrated the radome, got past the radar reflector, penetrated the dome-shaped pressure bulkhead and wound up in the cockpit, thus depressurizing the cabin.

The Electra cruises at about 350 knots and the kinetic energy of a duck at that speed is tremendous. It must have been a supercharged and pressurized duck with instrument rating to get up to 21,000 feet in night IFR. Ⓜ

Fortunate Crash

SHORTLY AFTER SUNRISE ONE FOGGY MORNING, YEARS AGO WHEN WE WERE STILL USING THE OLD FOUR-LEG A-N AURAL RADIO RANGES FOR NAVIGATION AND LOW APPROACHES, I DROVE TO THE POUGHKEEPSIE AIRPORT TO DO A LITTLE WORK ON MY PLANE.

I stopped in at the Flight Service Station and was told that an airplane had disappeared before daylight after being cleared for approach. As the sun was breaking up the fog, I was asked to fly out over the approach course in my Stinson Voyager to see whether I could locate a wreck.

The missing airplane was a Cessna 310 with pilot and three passengers aboard on a nonstop night flight from Chicago. It had been missing since before sunrise, about an hour and a half, in darkness and fog.

(The altitudes I am going to give here are not exact because the old approach procedure is long forgotten now. But they will be good for a description of what happened then.)

The range station was a few miles south of the field. Still farther south on the initial approach course to the station there were mountains, at 1,500 feet MSL. The airport is 165 feet MSL. The procedure turn and altitude over the station were at 2,500 feet to provide a 1,000-foot clearance over the hills. The terrain after passing the station was lower and the minimum approach altitude was about 400 feet above the field or possibly lower.

I took off and flew over the station southbound at 2,500 feet and went through the normal procedure turn for approach at 2,500 feet.

Just as I finished the turn, ahead of me I saw a swath mowed out of the second-growth trees on a gentle upward slope, and there was the wreck, at just about 1,500 feet above sea level. I then hastened to make some very low passes over it.

I could see no one in the airplane or around it, so I realized that the occupants had been taken away. I made a sketch of the faint roads and trails so I could later get to the wreck on foot. Then I landed back at the airport, drove my car up to the mountain and walked the trails to the airplane. Unfortunately, I did not go home first to get my camera.

What I saw were several surprises. First, the airplane had started to mow down the second-growth trees and the two tip tanks were torn off and left on the ground. That removed all of the fuel from the airplane and the danger of fire.

As the ground sloped upward and the airplane sloped downward, many parts were torn from the airplane and left along the route. Very little of the tail and wings remained on the airplane. The two engines, still running on carburetor fuel, had struck two large rocks squarely and the airplane's engines came to rest right on those rocks. Nothing else touched the ground—and they were the only rocks anywhere within 200 yards. (I looked.) Those two rocks had been lying there—ever since the great glacier brought them down from the Adirondack Mountains some 17,000 years ago—just waiting for that airplane.

The propellers had broken off and lay about 30 feet ahead. The nose of the plane was severely battered, and the beautiful brand-new Collins radios were a ruined mess. The landing gear was still retracted.

I could see no blood in the cabin. The Jeppesen manual was lying on the cockpit floor, open to the proper page showing the proper altitude for the approach. *But* the altimeter was set just 1,000 feet too low. The pilot probably thought he was at 2,500 feet but was actually at only 1,500 feet.

In those days, we used to set the altimeter for approach to zero at field level, the old Kollsman setting. That practice was no longer used in this country because it caused too many mistakes and crashes. I don't know whether that procedure had anything to do with the accident. The pilot was most likely tired and sleepy, having been flying nearly all night, 700 miles.

The most "fortunate" thing about this accident: The tip tanks were removed by the trees and prevented a fire. That's how I prefer the fuel—in tip tanks away from the fuselage. Ⓜ

Two Incidents at DCA

I N THE LATE 1950S I WAS FLYING FOUR DIFFERENT MODELS OF CONSTELLATIONS ENDING WITH THE SUPER-G. THEY WERE ALL THE LATEST TECHNOLOGY AND THE SUPER-G WAS A STRETCHED MODEL WITH A VERY LONG FUSELAGE.

Washington National Airport in the early 1960s

PHOTO COURTESY OF JOHN MILLER

. The airport terminal building at Washington National Airport faced east, overlooking the airport. There was an enormous window, so people inside could see all the runways. The control tower was on top of the terminal building. North/south Runway 1-19 was parallel to that big window and another runway, 33-5, crossed 1-19.

One fine morning, with scattered clouds at about 1,500 feet, the following incident took place in full view of people standing at that big observation window.

I had a totally full load of passengers and fuel in the Super-G, ready for a flight to Houston, Texas. I was cleared out to Runway 33, which was approximately three-fourths the length of Runway 1. While I was taxiing out, my copilot was looking in the manual and found that—with our load—we were not legal to take off on the shorter

Runway 33. So we were re-cleared to Runway 1, the longest. All other traffic was using 33 due to wind direction favoring it.

While I was busy taxiing out to Runway 1, my copilot determined from a chart what our V-1 (rotation) and V-2 (liftoff) speeds should be, with our weight, wind, temperature, etc. We then went through the takeoff checklist, ran up the four engines and were cleared for takeoff.

I opened the throttles to full takeoff power of the four big Wright 3350 compound engines. They growled loudly as the flight engineer made final adjustments of the settings of manifold pressures, rpms and syncronization.

I steered the nose wheel carefully along the runway centerline as the heavy airplane slowly accelerated, keeping my eye on the airspeed indicator as it crept up toward the V-1 speed. I was thinking about how I would lift the plane off at the V-2 speed and—after passing over the end of the runway, over the water— make a gentle left climbing turn to follow the Potomac River over the bridges and upstream past the Washington Monument and the Lincoln Memorial.

The airspeed indicator needle was almost to the V-1 speed when my right eye's peripheral vision through the copilot's window caught something moving. A quick look revealed a DC-4 on a takeoff roll on Runway 33 was about to exactly intercept the Constellation!

I could instantly see that it was closing in and not changing position in the frame of the window. There was no use trying to slow down, for we were very much too close to each other. There was only one thing to do: Lift off and drop the right wing to pass behind the DC-4. My airshow and military combat training and practice made that decision automatic.

I lifted the wheels off the pavement and dropped the right wingtip to almost scrape it. (The copilot told me later he was frozen with terror.) As I made the right bank-and-turn, the DC-4 passed directly in front of the nose of the Connie and the left wing actually passed over the tall rudder of the DC-4. In my radio headset, I could hear the tower operator calling the DC-4 pilot and saying, "Are you aware that you made an unauthorized takeoff?"

As we passed right across the path of the DC-4, behind it, I expected to get jolts from its four-propeller slipstream, but was surprised that I did not get any jolt at all, for I was slightly above it.

The whole event just seemed to be natural, as in combat practice or in airshow aerobatics. I have long been convinced that aerobatic training and practice is an important part of safety preparedness. If I had not had it, I would not have instinctively turned to pass *behind* the other airplane and kept my cool while doing so.

In the Marine Corps Reserve, long before WWII, we did a lot of air combat practice with the fighter biplanes, up to the Boeing F4B-4. Can anyone imagine what a horrible crash would have occurred right on National Airport? Having aerobatic fighter combat familiarity and in-grained habits really paid off!

As I climbed out and on upriver, entering the clouds to go on my way, I called the tower and said, "I'm not mad at anybody, just happy that we passed OK. Please keep it quiet. I will submit a report when I make the return trip."

I did so and then learned that the DC-4 was an Air Force aircraft that had returned from a night flight, discharged a load of military passengers and was then making the short hop to the Air Force base, right across the river from National.

I learned that the captain of the airplane was the safety officer at that air base. He had been flying at night, was tired, and he and his copilot had mistaken my clearance to take off as being for him.

On my return trip, I talked to the tower operators on the phone and they told me that many people in the terminal building had seen the whole "show" through that huge window and that two women had fainted! The news media had not been informed so there was no adverse publicity. If such an event happened today, there would be headlines all over the country.

Another very sad event occurred at National Airport that slightly involved me, also while I was flying a Constellation:

I was making a perfectly normal landing, to the north over the water at the south end of Runway 1. As I touched down and started to roll, I heard the tower operator excitedly say something about a crash and then call for emergency equipment.

A Bonanza had been cleared to land behind me and, as it came in over that same water, it suddenly rolled over inverted and crashed into the rocky, shallow water. The three people aboard were killed instantly. They were Mr. and Mrs. White and Mr. White's secretary. He was the owner of White Sewing Machines, I was told. At that time we had not learned to avoid the severe vortices of heavy airplanes.

Those of you who fly to the annual Oshkosh event on the first day know how close together we land, two or three at a time on the runway, right behind one another. A few years ago on the first day of heavy traffic at Oshkosh, I was landing my Bonanza on Runway 27 behind a P-51. The Bonanza suddenly rolled to at least a 60-degree right bank with the wingtip almost touching the ground. I barely recovered, using full aileron, and was very surprised that such a small airplane as a P-51 could cause such a strong vortice.

Not only was I shaken by the incident, my two passengers—my grandson and great-grandson—were also really "shook." Wingtip vortices can be very vicious, proportional to the aircraft weight but inversely to its speed. Ⓜ

> *I have long been convinced that aerobatic training and practice is an important part of safety preparedness.*

Updrafts and Downdrafts

IN THE LATE 1960S, I WAS TAKING OFF IN MY MODEL C BONANZA, POWERED BY THE MODEL E 185-205-HP ENGINE, AT BOULDER, COLORADO. MY LATE WIFE, DR. EDITH, WAS WITH ME. THE WEATHER WAS CLEAR, A PERFECT DAY. OUR TAKEOFF WAS DIRECTLY INTO THE WEST WIND. WE WERE HEADED OUT OVER THE CITY WITH HOUSES UNDER US AND TOWARD THE HIGH MOUNTAINS, A DISTANCE AWAY.

We barely missed hitting the tops of the houses, trying to get speed, which was difficult with the high angle of attack and its high drag. I really thought we were going to crash into the houses at full power—certain disaster.

Before reaching 300 feet above ground, the airspeed suddenly dropped off almost to the stall with the stall warning beeping incessantly. The airplane settled toward the housetops. The throttle was full open, the propeller in low pitch, properly, and the mixture had been adjusted to best power for the takeoff, due to the pressure altitude of the airport.

We barely missed hitting the tops of the houses, trying to get speed, which was difficult with the high angle of attack and its high drag. I really thought we were going to crash into the houses at full power—certain disaster.

By controlling the airspeed carefully, the speed very gradually increased as we barely missed the tops of the houses. Finally, I was able to get

some climb and turned left to parallel the mountains and get away. I was really drained by our narrow escape.

What had caused this near disaster? The answer is that a downdraft was caused by the wind coming over the mountain ridge and diving downward. As it dived toward the ground, it split so that part of it was flowing eastward toward the airport and the other part was flowing back toward the mountains, causing a rolling motion of the air, which was invisible, between the area of the split and the mountains.

We had flown first into the downdraft that caused the airplane to suddenly descend, then through the "split" or dead air, then into the tailwind.

I have done much flying in mountainous areas and am aware of

downdrafts, etc., but this one in the clear air took me by surprise anyway. I later learned that pilots flying at that airport have been aware of that phenomenon for a long time. I believe they make a quick turn after takeoff to avoid it.

On the evening before this occurrence, I was visiting an old friend in Boulder who was a sailplane pilot. He showed me some beautiful films of rolling cloud formations taken by a movie camera with time-lapse setting. The rolling clouds were formed by the west wind coming over the mountains—the very same condition I had encountered, but visible due to the cloud formations. From a pilot's standpoint, they were both beautiful and frightening.

He told me about an adventure he had a few years before. He was towed off from Boulder with the intention of making a nonstop round trip in the sailplane to Cheyenne, Wyoming, for a record.

The weather was severe clear, but a strong wind was blowing from the west. He caught a good updraft that turned out to be a lot better than expected. The sailplane was carried upward at better than 2,000 fpm—much faster than his glide could descend.

Quickly, he was at such a high altitude that he had to use oxygen, and the updraft continued carrying him to the startling altitude of more that 40,000 feet.

With only summer clothing, he was suffering severely from the extreme cold. If oxygen had not been available, he would have had to bail out to save his life.

By the time he was able to glide downward, he was nearer Cheyenne than Boulder. So he called the Cheyenne tower to tell them he was at some 35,000 feet descending to land—with an emergency, almost out of oxygen and nearly frozen.

The tower operators could not believe such an altitude (airliners were not flying that high before jets), but he finally convinced them. By the time he landed, about an hour after his peak altitude, quite a crowd had gathered to see his arrival. He called for his friends to drive his trailer up to Cheyenne to transport him and the sailplane home. His altitude was recorded officially on his barograph but it was by no means a world record. Sailplanes have gone even higher than that.

This experience shows how powerful those updrafts and downdrafts can be in the Rocky Mountain areas. For each updraft, there must be a downdraft. Even in the absence of any strong wind, there can be strong thermal vertical drafts that can be dangerous. (M)

An updraft in 1960s took a sailplane to 40,000 feet out of Boulder, Colorado. The pilot drew a crowd as he glided to an emergency landing in a field near Cheyenne, Wyoming.

Hypoxia Confessions

IN MILITARY AIRPLANES, BEFORE WWII, SOMETIMES I FLEW AT ALTITUDES AS HIGH AS 18,000 FEET FOR FORMATION-FLYING PRACTICE WITHOUT OXYGEN, BECAUSE WE DID NOT HAVE OXYGEN EQUIPMENT IN OUR USMCR SQUADRON AIRPLANES. HOWEVER, WHEN DOING TACTICAL FORMATION FLYING FOR ONLY A FEW MINUTES, OUR FORMATION FLYING BECAME ROUGH AND DANGEROUS BECAUSE OF HYPOXIA, SO WE SPLIT UP AND DIVED TO LOWER ALTITUDES. THOSE PILOTS WHO WERE CIGARETTE SMOKERS OR THOSE WHO HAD BEEN DRINKING THE NIGHT BEFORE, WERE THE FIRST TO GET ERRATIC IN THEIR FLYING.

My wife remarked that the hotel carpets in Mexico City did not look very well vacuumed. I told her vacuum cleaners don't work very well at 7,300 feet. That's why they use those old-fashioned carpet sweepers. Even vacuum cleaners get hypoxia!

When flying across the continent in my own Baron at 21,000 or 22,000 feet, my late wife Edith and I always had oxygen. On one occasion at night, however, we had a passenger who I checked periodically. On one of those checks I could not wake her up and discovered that her oxygen hose had become disconnected. She was elderly and it was certainly fortunate that I caught the discrepancy in time.

One time in my Bonanza I flew to 22,500 feet solo to test for autogas vaporlock. It did not occur but I returned to low altitude promptly.

On a trip to Mexico City in my C35, we arrived with the main tanks almost empty but with a 20-gallon auxiliary tank full of autogas. We decided to fly up to the summit of the volcano Popocatepetl, 17,888 feet, which was snowcapped and throwing steam or smoke at the time. We circled it once and took photos at 18,500 feet. We did not have oxygen but were up there only briefly before landing at Mexico City Airport, which is at 7,300 feet.

In the hotel later, Edith remarked that the carpets in the hallways did not look very well vacuumed. I told her vacuum cleaners don't work very well at 7,300 feet. That's why they use those old-fashioned carpet sweepers. Even vacuum cleaners get hypoxia!

When I was flying for UAL in the 1930s in the Boeing 247-D twin-engine airliner on the transcontinental route, we flew across the high country from Cheyenne, Wyoming, to Salt Lake City, Utah. That stretch was a veritable ice factory!

The minimum IFR altitude was 10,000 feet. Sometimes, in fact more often than not, we flew at higher altitudes to avoid rough clouds or icing in clouds, often going as high at 15,000 feet and some trips actually went to 17,000 feet for at least a brief time to avoid the tops of icing clouds. Pressurization had not been developed at that time and we were not supplied with oxygen.

I remember one night I heard a passenger, deplaning at SLC, say that he slept all the way from Cheyenne. Not surprising at 15,000 feet! Pilots who were smokers could not tolerate such altitudes. On EAL, years later in the DC-3s, I had copilots and passengers who were cigarette smokers pass out at altitudes of 13,000 feet or higher when I was trying to get over weather, before we were finally limited to 8,000 feet.

Smokers beware! My copilots passed out suddenly in those cases. If flying alone, it could be very dangerous for a solo pilot. High altitudes are dangerous territory. I have strong suspicions that many CFIT (Controlled Flight Into Terrain) accidents have been caused by pilots who could not think clearly due to hypoxia.

I have had several other experiences with hypoxia. One occurred during a WWII test flight. I was at 16,000 feet running a series of tests on an amphibian when I began talking to myself—a lot of nonsense. For instance, I remember saying that on the previous test flight I had forgotten to put the landing gear down, but could not seem to remember the results, so kept on trying to recall it and assumed that I would catch hell when I landed this time.

I finally looked at the oxygen meter and it read zero, with everything turned on properly. I dived for a lower altitude, flew around at about 1,500 feet, until I felt well enough to make a safe landing. I had been re-breathing my own breath in the mask. It turned out to be a case of sabotage by some Hitler admirer who had deliberately crushed an oxygen tube or some other trick. I never did hear the details of the investigation.

Another incident was much more serious. While flying for EAL at LaGuardia (now JFK), I accepted a Constellation with a load of passengers that had only one of its two pressurization systems in working order. The one operable system worked OK as far as the scheduled stop in Atlanta. During climbout from there to 20,000 feet, the flight engineer had great difficulty with the pressurization. He finally told me he had gotten it stabilized and it was holding at 10,000 feet cabin altitude, at 20,000 feet cruising altitude and that was the best he could do.

It was rough during the climb so I was busy flying, and then barely on top it was smooth air. I did not wish to go down 2,000 feet to get 8,000-foot cabin altitude because the clouds below me were very rough. It was a very late night trip to Houston and San Antonio. The engineer and copilot dozed off, as usual on that scheduled late night flight. We were on autopilot. I watched everything (I thought) and ate apples to keep myself occupied and awake on the smooth direct-line flight. I never drink coffee. It always made my crew members sleepier after the first drink or two.

There were none of the later automatic drop-down passenger masks in that early Constellation. After a while one of the stewardesses came to the cockpit wearing a mask and a walk-around oxygen cylinder. She said the other girl was asleep and so were all of the passengers as usual, but that she felt woozy. I told her the cabin altitude was at 10,000 feet

The engineer and copilot dozed off, as usual on that scheduled late night flight. We were on autopilot. I watched everything (I thought) and ate apples to keep myself occupied and awake on the smooth direct-line flight.

Capt. John Miller, copilot "Tack" Marshall and engineer Oakes at 6,000 feet at night in Super Constellation #213.

instead of the normal 8,000 feet and not to worry. I later noticed that my hands were a little weak and remembered my previous event in the amphibian when that had occurred, so attributed it to the extra 2,000 feet of cabin altitude to 10,000 feet for a long time.

Why didn't I go down to a lower altitude regardless of the rougher air? I don't know, other than I was already hypoxic and had become unable to think of it. I was in the ingrained habit of flying that trip at 20,000

103

feet. I then woke up the engineer and asked him for a mask, out of reach for me. He gave me one, all sterilized and sealed in a transparent plastic bag. I had real difficulty with my weak hands, getting it open, only to find that it was the wrong type that did not have provision for my boom microphone, so asked for another.

I finally had to puncture that bag with my pencil, my hands getting still weaker. I did not seem to feel sleepy with all that activity. With oxygen, I brightened up quickly.

It then dawned on me to actually look at the cabin altimeter, which was located inconveniently in the riser under the doorstep from the cabin door behind us. I struggled around in my seat to see it with a flashlight. It showed almost 20,000 feet cabin altitude! We had been at that cabin altitude for fully one and three-fourths hours! There was a red warning light next to it but it was dead, as was its illuminating light. That was why the engineer had misread the altimeter (he was probably weakened quickly, being a smoker). I was busy with the flying, getting up out of the rough clouds and setting up for level cruise. Evidently, due to hypoxia, he thought the cabin pressure was stabilized because it actually was, due to the climb ending. I had lost some cognition, too, without realizing it,

due to onset of hypoxia.

I called the center on the radio and announced a pressurization loss and an immediate emergency descent to 6,000 feet. There was no traffic and by that time no clouds below me. I was cleared immediately but hadn't even waited for it.

The stewardess came forward to say that some of the passengers were complaining of ear pains, so I slowed the descent but told her to let me know whether anyone did not wake up at all. I was afraid that some passenger might have tobacco lungs or a weak heart.

When I leveled off at 6,000 feet, the autopilot suddenly failed, possibly due to the rapid descent or just a coincidence. It was difficult for me to get back to accurate hand-flying until I had oxygen for about a half hour.

That incident could have been prevented by an aural warning in our headsets that the cabin altitude was too high, using the same switch as for the warning light. But if it was the switch at fault, that would not work either.

At that time smoking by the passengers and crew was permitted. The smoke-filled air passed out through a pressure-operated pop valve to keep the cabin pressure constant. As the smoke-polluted air passed rapidly out through the narrow opening of the valve, a coating of tobacco smoke—sticky, stinky

goo—was deposited on the mating surfaces of the valve, an unbelievable nasty mess. That caused the valve to stick closed until the cabin pressure built up enough above normal to pop it open. Then the pressure of the cabin would take a sudden drop until the valve closed. Those repetitive changes in pressure were called "bumps." After smoking was prohibited, the problem disappeared.

One time I was flying my Bonanza from Spearfish, South Dakota, to Jackson, Wyoming, to land at Jackson Hole Airport. There was a solid wall of thunderstorms along the 12,000-foot ridge on the east side of the valley, so I turned around and landed at Worland, Wyoming, a farming town. It was late afternoon on a Saturday. I was given the use of a courtesy car and drove to town at dusk.

After checking in at a motel, I went out looking for something to eat, for I had not had anything since breakfast at Spearfish. Restaurants were not plentiful there, so I settled for the best one I could find, not a gem. The food was so poor I couldn't finish it, so went back to the motel to bed, still hungry, anticipating an early start on Sunday morning to avoid thunderstorm build-ups, as advised by Flight Service.

I had an important appointment to speak to an audience at Jackson. I

awoke before daylight Sunday morning and found the town was securely shut down—not a single human being anywhere and no restaurant open. I did not seem extremely hungry so drove to the airport. The FBO was locked up and could not get to the candy machine. So I took off while the weather was perfect for the relatively short flight. I felt fine, empty but no severe hunger.

I had a "papoose" oxygen kit strapped to the back of the RH seat, but had never, ever had any trouble flying across the continent at 12,500 feet altitude. On reaching that altitude, however, I began to feel very woozy and almost dizzy. With the top of the ridge only 500 feet below me, I had to pay attention to flying but put on the oxygen mask and tried to open the valve. My hand and arm were too weak to budge it and I was getting more woozy and dizzy.

I removed the shoulder harness straps so I could move to get a better advantage but still could not open the valve. I felt I was about to pass out, so put the lap belt back on, leaving the shoulder straps until later.

I passed over the ridge and started to descend down the valley toward Jackson Hole Airport. The airport level was at 6,447 feet, only 6,000 feet lower, but I thought the lower altitude would give me some relief. I tried to talk on the radio but my voice was slurred and apparently the Unicom operator could not understand me.

I could not find the windsock when circling but saw one small plane land to the south so made a left downwind approach, still at about 7,500 feet pattern altitude. I put the gear down and tried to make the appropriate announcements on the radio with my slurred voice.

On approach to the runway, I was undershooting severely toward a steep downward slope of the ground right at the beginning of the runway. I tried to push open that miserable knob throttle, but my hand was too weak to squeeze the knob to unlock it, much less push it. In desperation I took my left hand off the control wheel and used both hands to get the throttle open barely in time (the prop was still in high pitch). The plane slammed down on the very beginning of the runway without help from me, or damage.

From the moment I gave that throttle the push I was so exhausted I was helpless, yet I could see what was going on. The airplane made a 45-degree turn to the left, off the runway, down a deep swale, up across the taxiway, off the unfenced airport into a brushy area, still with the throttle wide open but the prop still in high pitch.

All during that time, I kept saying to myself, "Why doesn't it slow down?" but did not have any volition to do anything. I fully realized that the airplane would eventually strike some rough spot and be wrecked but still just sat there like a bewildered passenger until it finally happened. The nose wheel struck a depression, collapsed and the airplane turned over on its back violently.

Without the shoulder straps, my forehead hit the lightly padded edge of the glare shield and that bent my neck back against its forward-bend set, due to my age. Hanging, inverted from my seat belt, the blood pressure to my brain increased and immediately revived me. I clearly recall saying aloud, "I'm going to burn and I deserve it."

The roof of the cabin was crushed so far down that when I released my seat belt there was little room for me to struggle or get out of the broken left window. I was locked in an inverted position with my weight on my head and my feet upward.

Fortunately for me, there was a conference of the Flying Physicians to start the next morning, and some of them had already landed. Several rushed to the wreck and managed to get me out of that left window that had been crushed to half its size. When they first arrived, I heard one of them say, "I could tell he was hypoxic by his voice."

I realized that the airplane would eventually strike a rough spot and wreck, but I still just sat there like a bewildered passenger until it finally happened. The nose wheel struck a depression, collapsed, and the airplane turned over on its back violently.

I was taken to the hospital in an ambulance where I spent a week under observation and partly recovering from a painful neck, two partially blackened eyes and a broken rib.

The physicians told me the combination of hypoxia and hypoglycemia was a deadly combination and I was fortunate to survive long enough to guide the plane to the airport. I lost the opportunity to speak at the convention and also lost a fine airplane, but I was very fortunate to not lose my life. I'm now more careful to carry emergency food in the airplane and not to fly in a half-starved condition.

A few weeks later I had another Bonanza, thanks to Avemco. I have made several transcontinental trips since then with no trouble at 11,000 or 12,000. But I did wear a mask and breathed oxygen for at least half an hour before arriving at my destinations, or temporarily above 10,000 feet due to MEA sections of airways.

There have been several incidents in which pressurization has been lost unnoticed with fatal crashes resulting. Pressurization loss is insidious, as is the loss of oxygen flow, so of course a lurking danger.

I flew the Douglas DC-8 for five years before retirement, the first jet operated by EAL, a truly fine airplane. At high altitudes at least one pilot had to be wearing a mask and actually breathing oxygen. The other pilot and the engineer had to have masks hanging on their necks, connected and ready.

I hope that my experiences and confessions will serve as warnings to my fellow members of the American Bonanza Society, and others as well, for many are flying turbocharged airplanes at increasingly high altitudes—treacherous territory.

And just remember: Those who smoke are much more susceptible to loss of consciousness at high altitude. Those who drink alcohol are at risk because the lower pressure at altitude causes the alcohol in the blood to vaporize and create intoxication that would not occur at lower altitudes.

Unusual Sights—but No UFOs

I HAVE DONE A LOT OF FLYING SINCE SOLOING IN DECEMBER 1923—ABOUT FOUR SOLID YEARS—BUT ONE THING I HAVE NEVER SEEN IS A TORNADO. I HAVE SEEN THE DAMAGE CAUSED BY THEM WHEN FLYING OVER THEIR PATHS AFTER THEY WERE LONG GONE. THEY OFTEN CREATE UNBELIEVABLY TOTAL DESTRUCTION, SOMETIMES EVEN LEAVING THE GROUND BARE OF GRASS. BELIEVE ME, I HAVE NO DESIRE TO BE NEAR ENOUGH TO SEE ONE FROM THE GROUND, WHERE ESCAPE MIGHT NOT BE POSSIBLE.

The tower operator said excitedly that they were abandoning the tower immediately because in the lightning flashes they could see two tornado funnels coming across the airport.

In an airplane, it would probably be possible to fly away from one, but if flying on instruments, you might contact one inadvertently and be destroyed.

If I were to live in tornado territory, I think I would live uneasily unless in a steel re-enforced solid concrete building with inch-thick windows like portholes. However, I have witnessed several rather interesting phenomena of meteorology worth writing about.

The closest I ever came to a tornado while flying was one night at 6,000 feet, about 5,000 feet above ground in a Constellation on instruments in a thunderstorm with lots of lightning and turbulence. I was passing over Austin (Texas) Airport on my way to San Antonio and was talking to the Austin Tower about my flight conditions.

The tower operator said excitedly that they were abandoning the tower immediately because in the lightning flashes they could see two tornado funnels coming across the airport. I did not feel anything other than the same turbulence I had before, although I was apparently right above the funnels. The tower operator came back on the radio later and said that some aircraft had been damaged on the airport.

In 1932 I was in Louisville, Kentucky, to participate in an airshow by the American Air Aces team of pilots. One of our late United Flying Octogenarians*

(UFO) members, Clyde Ice, was there as the oldest member of the team. I was the youngest member and now am the only survivor. The other team members were Johnny Livingston, Art Davis, Len Povey, Art Killups—all wonderful aerobatic pilots but only memories now. All died natural deaths except Killups who was killed in 1933. In those days there were not as many regulations as now, and we put on some wild shows.

I was on the airport getting ready for the show to start the next day. It was a hot but dry day. We saw a huge dark wall of clouds approaching from the northwest, a cold front. But we did not know that much about meteorology at that time, so did not have a name for it.

Visibility was very good and we saw the dark wall of cloud coming from a long distance away. There was an astonishing thing in advance of the cloud bank—a huge, perfectly formed roll cloud, parallel and in advance of the dark wall of cloud. It extended out of sight northeast and southwest and was rolling like a huge shaft, forward at its bottom and backwards at its top.

I took off in my Pitcairn PCA-2 autogiro and climbed rapidly toward it. I judged it about 500 feet in diameter, rolling quite rapidly. It was perfectly formed, cylindrical as a huge pipeline and extended in both directions curved out over the horizon in a straight line.

As I approached it in very clear air at about 4,000 feet above ground, I was lifted rapidly by a strong updraft at about 3,000 feet per minute at idle power and more than the vertical speed indicator could read. I was quickly lifted above 8,000 feet before I decided that it would be a good idea to get out of there and back to the airport and a tie-down before the dark wall cloud got to the airport.

I actually had difficulty getting down because of the updraft in advance of the roll cloud, but made it just before the strong wind struck, kicking up clouds of dust. I got tied down before the wind struck the autogiro. There was no rain or lightning as the front passed over us. That roll cloud was beautiful in its perfection.

Once safely on the ground, I was asked whether I had seen an Aeronca C-3 that had also taken off to observe the roll cloud. I was told there were two men in that frail little 36-hp plane and they had disappeared in the high altitude in that strong updraft. When last seen, they were far above the roll cloud and had passed over the huge dark frontal cloud and out of sight. No one had radios in those days, so their friends were understandably worried.

Strangely, there was no rain during the frontal passage and the clouds began to break up afterward to still clearer air. A tiny speck appeared in a big hole in the clouds to the relief of everyone on the ground. The Aeronca landed fully an hour after its disappearance.

The two men had quite a ride to 18,000 feet and nearly froze. They were barely above the frontal cloud at the 18,000-foot level and then the cloud began to break up so that they could spiral down through the hole. That must have been a world-record altitude for a 36-hp Aeronca C-3.

They said they were completely helpless in the strong updraft— 18,000 feet is much too high to fly without oxygen. Luckily, they were not lifted higher. They were fortunate in not being caught in the down draft behind the roll cloud, for that would have taken them down into the high wind and they could not have gotten on the ground before it struck the airport.

One early morning, shortly before sunrise, I was flying a DC-3 south from Jacksonville, Florida. Looking to the east out over the ocean, there was a beautiful comet barely above the horizon and just above the sun, which was still below the horizon. There was a veil of light around the forward side of the nucleus and trailing back to form a double tail.

I had never heard of a veiled comet before, but was told later by an astronomer that I had called it a veil correctly. It was a beautiful sight, but I did not have a camera. Within five minutes, the sun came up above the horizon and the comet was then invisible.

One winter night I was flying a DC-8 southwest from New York to Houston at 35,000 feet. We were on top of a solid cloud layer under brilliant stars when I noticed what appeared to be a contrail above me. I suddenly realized, however, that it was not a contrail at all. It was a huge comet, pointing toward the sun which had set hours before. It had a tremendously long tail.

I got EAL to patch me on the radio to the National Observatory in Washington, D.C., and the astronomer there told me they were very disappointed that the solid overcast prevented them from seeing it. It had been discovered simultaneously by two amateur astronomers, one from the United States and the other from Japan. It had been named for them by combining parts of their names into a single word, but I forget now what it is. Ⓜ

United Flying Octogenarians

About 1987, a group of 80-plus-year-old pilots had a little fly-in to a small airport in California. While there, we decided to start a club especially for aviators who attained the age of 80 or more and were still flying. We named it the United Flying Octogenarians.

When we realized its three initials were those used for fictitious flying saucers, unidentified flying objects, we thought it would be fun to have a membership button made with the initials UFO superimposed on the image of a flying saucer and that became the logo for our club. The idea quickly caught on and octogenarian pilots began to join just for the fun of it and for the distinction of being a member of such an unusual and exclusive aviators' organization.

Three years later, there were so many members that an annual meeting was held in California where the actual formalization of the club was made. Officers were elected and I served as president for 15 years.

Nonagenarian Nomad

SEPTEMBER 8, 2000, I TOOK OFF FROM POUGHKEEPSIE, NEW YORK, ON AN IFR FLIGHT PLAN IN MY V35A, N19WC, (WILD COWBOY) TO TERRE HAUTE, INDIANA, FOR THE FIRST LEG OF MY *ALMOST* ANNUAL FLIGHT TO THE AMERICAN BONANZA SOCIETY CONVENTION—THIS ONE IN SAN ANTONIO—THEN ON TO THE WEST COAST.

John Miller at Stinson Field, arriving for the ABS Convention in San Antonio

Before entering the clouds, both comm transmitters failed and I returned to the ground. After more than an hour of work by the avionics shop, they started to work again. I made it to Terre Haute before sunset to visit a relative. After three days, I continued on to Stinson Field in San Antonio without event.

Years ago, after WWII, I flew a regular Eastern Air Lines schedule to SAT from NY. San Antonio was a "cow town" then but is enormous now, and the many friends I made there have all flown west to the forever. The schedule started with DC-4s, then DC-7, Constellations, Lockheed Electra L-188 four-engine turboprop and finally with the DC-8 four-engine jet.

During that time, I witnessed the deliberate destruction of thousands of beautiful AT-6 trainers, flown to Stinson Field in formations from all over the United States, just to prevent them from getting on the market. Distressing! Many carloads of spare parts were included and destroyed.

At the ABS Convention I was given a beautiful and unique award by the ABS, the Airmanship Award, sincerely appreciated. I carried it on the rest of my trip.

After the convention, my next stop was Tucson, passing over El Paso, which was a little town when

I first flew there in 1931. It is astoundingly big now and looks like the entire population of Mexico has moved to ELP.

At Tucson, I visited the huge Pima Air Museum especially to again see the Columbia-Grumman XJL-1 amphibian on which I ran the tests during WWII. Only two were built before the war ended.

Then a short hop to Phoenix for an overnight visit with a daughter-in-law and the next day I flew to El Monte, California, for a visit with a niece, the daughter of my late brother. After only one night there, I hopped over the mountains to visit one of my granddaughters and her husband and three of my great grandchildren at Bakersfield. Stayed there several days taking them to restaurants, etc.

The flight from Bakersfield to Aurora, Oregon, is over some of the most rugged mountainous territory in the United States. The snow-capped domes of Lassen Peak, Mt. Shasta and Mt. Hood glistened in the sun far above me. In the distance, Mount St. Helens pierced the horizon, but it didn't erupt for me. All so familiar, but I might never see them again.

Getting to Aurora required a clearance down through the clouds but the comms went on strike again, both of them at the same time, just as before at Poughkeepsie. The ground stations could not read my transmissions, which were chopped up into little pieces.

I turned back to stay overnight at Medford, Oregon, but diverted to take photos of Crater Lake again. The crater was surrounded by a pretty circle of clouds, but I got one photo from 12,500 feet. I always love to fly around that beautiful crater. On a clear day, with the sun high, the mineral-laden lake is a beautiful kaleidoscope of changing colors as a plane circles it.

Years ago, when landing at Medford, it was a small grass field. But now it is a busy airport, including helicopter training. When I touched down (gently), the radios came back to life, but it had to be RON.

The next day was clear to Aurora, but the radios became unintelligible again. To compound the trouble, the landing gear motor failed. So I cranked it down by hand—51 turns, counterclockwise, quite stiff toward the end.

I was astonished at Aurora Airport, where many corporate planes are based. It has one fine long runway and enormous new hangars with more being built. In one, the good mechanics removed the gear motor and the next day I was given a ride to the Portland Airport where an accessory shop is located. The elderly mechanic repaired the motor in less than an hour. The only trouble was a worn commutator and brushes. I have done the same job a number of times in my own shop on my lathe on other Bonanza landing gear and flap motors.

The shop at Aurora reinstalled the motor and ran several retractions. The avionics shop worked several hours but could not locate the trouble with the comms because they were working perfectly again. Those three bills came to about $1,300.

During about a week's visit with a daughter-in-law and a grandson, we visited two museums, one at McMinnville where the Howard Hughes' HK-1 "Spruce Goose" is being surrounded by a new museum building. The wings and tail were off and being reconditioned. The tailplane alone was, I think, about a 100-foot span!

That flying boat is the largest ever built and has eight P&W R-4360, 3,000-hp engines. I'm a seaplane and flying boat pilot and would love to fly it. I had seen it in

---

I witnessed the deliberate destruction of thousands of beautiful AT-6 trainers, flown to Stinson Field in formations from all over the United States, just to prevent them from getting on the market. Distressing!

its former display hangar at Long Beach. It's bigger than some ships.

There is a very large and active pilots' club at Aurora, some 250 members, and they have built a huge and beautiful clubhouse on the airport. The sculptured entrance door alone cost more than $10,000. I was a guest there during one of their meetings. A friendlier bunch of pilots never existed.

The next hop was to Salt Lake City, very familiar to me for many years. The route took me over Prom-

---

I visited a huge research facility where a new rotorcraft is being developed, the Groen Brothers gyroplane. It is to be a passenger and cargo-carrier aircraft. It is not a helicopter but will jump off and land in extremely limited areas at much lower cost than the expensive helicopters.

---

ontory Point where the two rail lines of the first transcontinental railroad joined together from each direction in 1869, but I was in the clouds so couldn't see it this time.

When I was flying the Pitcairn autogiro, and the Boeing 247-D for UAL, and my own planes in the 1930s to the present time, I flew into SLC often. It is much, much larger now. This flight was IFR so I could get only glimpses down through the clouds during vectors to the ILS for landing on the old north runway on the east side of the field, ignoring the two new longer, parallel airline runways which I used with my 56TC Baron.

At Salt Lake, I visited for several days with an old friend who was the chief engineer at Columbia Aircraft Corporation at Valley Stream, Long Island, New York, during WWII when I was his chief test pilot. We had a great talk-fest about old flying and designing times before WWII.

In addition, I visited a huge research facility where a new rotorcraft is being developed, the Groen Brothers gyroplane. It is to be a passenger and cargo-carrier aircraft. It is not a helicopter but will jump off and land in extremely limited areas at much lower cost than the expensive helicopters.

The next flight was from SLC

to Spearfish, South Dakota, over the mountains and several big mining towns. Some of the mountains had snow on their tops already. At Spearfish I visited an old friend with whose father I did a lot of exhibition flying in 1932. He has a lovely home just west of Spearfish in Wyoming, surrounded on three sides by a creek full of big trout. I saw his father fly perfectly during his big 100th birthday party, attended by 500 people in 1989 at Spearfish. He lived past 103, flying from 1921—two years before I soloed.

From Spearfish it was just a routine flight home with an overnight stop at Kankakee, Illinois, and an IFR from there to Poughkeepsie on October 10, 32 days after departure. I took a photo of the ice on the left wing during the instrument descent from 11,000 feet. The tour totaled approximately 5,500 nm.

All during the 49:22 flying time, including side trips, the IO-520 engine shed not a drop of oil in the cowling and never missed a beat. But the comm radios gave no end of trouble, evidently originating in the audio panel wiring or switches, since it intermittently affected both comms simultaneously. The ground stations would say, "Your radios are awful, 98 percent unreadable. Please get them fixed." I will, or use an axe!

Coast to Coast, Again

IN MAY 1931—WHEN AIR NAVIGATION WAS BY PENCIL LINES DRAWN ON RAND MCNALLY STATE MAPS SHOWING KNOWN AIRFIELDS, ISOGONAL LINES AND ELEVATIONS— I MADE THE FIRST TRANSCONTINENTAL FLIGHTS IN EACH DIRECTION IN AN AUTOGIRO—FORBEAR OF THE HELICOPTER.

The flight was made to prove that not only was the autogiro practical, it was safe. I had no sectional charts, aviation weather reports, paved runways, aviation radio for communication and very little information about the available airports.

To celebrate the anniversary of that flight 70 years ago, I just couldn't resist doing it again, this time in my V35A Bonanza, N19WC (one-nine-wild-cowboy). So on July 20, 2001, I set out from Poughkeepsie, New York (POU), with a forecast of good weather, headed for Oshkosh to the 2001 EAA annual event.

Within 30 minutes after takeoff, I found myself on instruments in very rough air. After about two hours, the autopilot started oscillating the control wheel. Evidently the motor was overheated due to the extra heavy work, so I turned it off and flew by hand for about an hour. Then the autopilot

worked OK again. That was not the first time it had happened.

The very rough air continued all the way to Lake Michigan, then the weather cleared and I made a visual approach to OSH where I met a number of friends in the ABS tent.

After OSH I visited friends at Minneapolis, who took me to a private aviation museum at the nearby Anoka Airport. When I walked in, I recognized one airplane as one I had flown at Teterboro Airport, New Jersey, in 1930. It was a Stinson high-wing, fabric-covered cabin monoplane with a Packard nine-cylinder radial air-cooled diesel engine.

I made the mistake of thinking it was the one that made a record nonrefueling endurance record in 1929. I also remembered a photo being taken of me after flying the record-making airplane there at Teterboro in 1930. When I found

John Miller, Roger Williams and "Col." Julian at Teterboro Airport in 1930, with the Packard diesel-powered Bellanca that set a world record for a non-refueling endurance flight.

the photo, however, it was of me and the Bellanca monoplane that actually made the endurance record. (I had flown both of them, but my memory had slipped a little.) That endurance record was not broken until several years after WWII.

I don't know what became of the Bellanca endurance airplane, but its flight proved the endurance and economy of the Packard diesel

Stinson high-wing, with a Packard nine-cylinder radial air-cooled diesel engine

Kansas Aviation Museum volunteer Mary VanScyoc, the first female control tower operator, points out a picture of John in the book Prairie Runways. The photo in the book was taken in 1931 when he stopped at Wichita Municipal Airport on his transcontinental flight.

engine. I think diesel engines may someday take over general aviation light aircraft powerplants.

The next stop was at Wichita, Kansas, where I visited the American Bonanza Society headquarters and the Kansas Aviation Museum adjacent to McConnell AFB. The museum occupies a facility that was formerly the Wichita Municipal Airport where I stopped on my flight in 1931.

While I was there, I visited with Mary VanScyoc, the first U.S. female air traffic controller who works at the museum as a volunteer. She took me on a tour that included the control tower where she had worked before WWII. I saw restored airplanes and parts and pieces of other airplanes that I had flown many years ago.

When I left Wichita, I flew to a private field at Pecan Plantation east of Granbury, Texas, to visit Gene Keyt, a well-known ABS member who had invited me to speak to their local EAA Chapter—in an air-conditioned hangar!

Then I made a seven-hour hop to Gillespie Field in San Diego. The people at the San Diego Air & Space Museum interviewed me on tape about the 1931 flight that landed at the North Island NAS on May 28, 1931, before any of the personnel at the museum had been born! There are photos of the 1931 event at the museum and at the NAS.

The autogiro created quite a stir wherever it landed. Even schools— and some factories—closed to allow the people to see it. At that time, there was great promise that the autogiro would be the answer to personal flying. Its descendant has never lived up to that prediction, mainly due to its great expense. Nevertheless, it is an extremely successful aircraft type.

After visiting relatives at Arcadia, California, and a granddaughter and great-grandchildren at Bakersfield, I made a six-hour flight over the most rugged territory in the USA at 11,000 feet. I stopped overnight in Liberal, Kansas, then made a four-hour flight to visit a relative at Terre Haute, Indiana. Another four-hour IFR flight took me back to my home in Poughkeepsie.

This flight across the continent, with two fuel stops, totaled only 14 hours of flying. I have Beryl D'Shannon tip tanks to carry a total of 110 gallons of fuel. In the past I have made the eastbound flight with only one stop by my usual back-side-of-lean flying (lean of peak).

On all of this tour, my Bonanza used only 13.3 gph at cruise on back-side-of-lean with the new GAMIjectors in my Continental IO-520-A engine. Because no one will believe it, I hesitate to even mention that, in the entire 35.5 hours of flying, only one quart of oil was used.

John Miller's V35A Bonanza, N19WC (One-Nine-Wild-Cowboy)

John Miller watches as Loreta J.R. Mead Almond, a member of Wichita's Women's Aero, christens his aircraft "Missing Link" on May 24, 1931.

Visiting Kitty Hawk

I WAS INVITED TO ATTEND THE 98TH ANNIVERSARY CELEBRATION OF THE WRIGHT BROTHERS FIRST FLIGHTS ON DECEMBER 17, 1903, AT KITTY HAWK.

John Miller in 2000 at the base of the Wright Brothers Monument on Kill Devil Hill at Kitty Hawk, North Carolina

PHOTO COURTESY OF JOHN MILLER

Due to the large number of people expected, I was privileged to stay at the home of an active pilot who lives not far from the activities, a really generous man.

On December 16, 2001, the day after my 96th birthday, the weather was perfect and I flew my Bonanza, N19WC (Wild Cowboy), VFR to Manteo Airport, nearest to Kitty Hawk. The FBO (County Airport Authority) treated me royally and put my Bonanza in a hangar for the three nights I stayed over.

My host and a friend of his took me on a tour of the site of the first flights at Kill Devil Hill and the beautiful, impressive monument atop the hill, which is actually a huge sand dune now stabilized by grass plantings. The original glider experimental flights were made down that hill. The first powered flights were made from the foot of the hill over flat territory.

There are smaller monuments, showing the starts of the first flights and the landing spots of each flight. Actually, a baseball player could easily bat a ball farther than those flights, but they were flights nevertheless.

When I was flying back and forth, NY-MIA, as a captain on Eastern Air Lines, I passed over the site many times without seeing it due to height, fog or darkness. I was tremendously impressed, especially by the monument.

The museum at the site is currently being enlarged, so only a replica of the original "flyer" was on display; the other items are in storage. There is an excellent runway next to the hill and I shall certainly land there for another visit when the museum work is finished. I strongly advise others to land and visit.

The ceremonies were impressive and there was a luncheon and a banquet, with speeches, of course. I was presented with a finely framed print of that famous photograph of Orville Wright making one of the first flights, with his brother Wilbur running alongside the right wingtip. The original glass plate photo is in the Smithsonian.

Kill Devil Hill overlooks the spot where the first flights were made for our now wonderful ability to fly, after thousands of centuries of man's envy of the birds. We just happened to be born in the first century of flight. Think of that!

My return flight was also in fair weather but IFR and I was routed right over Kennedy Airport at 7,000 feet. It is hard for me to believe that it is now almost 40 years since I was last flying there with the DC-8 jets, only six decades after the Wright flights! I'll go back to Kitty Hawk for the 100th anniversary in 2003.

My CFI via Computer

FOR DECADES I ATTENDED REFRESHER COURSES EVERY TWO YEARS TO CONTINUE MY FLIGHT INSTRUCTOR RATING. THE COURSE PROVIDED BY AOPA AT ALBANY, NEW YORK, REQUIRED A ROUND TRIP BY CAR OF ABOUT 170 MILES AND AN OVERNIGHT STAY AT A HOTEL FOR TWO NIGHTS, PLUS MEALS—AN EXPENSIVE PROCEDURE. IT ALSO INVOLVED THE RISK OF MISSING THE COURSE DUE TO ILLNESS OR OTHER MISFORTUNE AND THUS THE LOSS OF THE RATING.

In 2001 I took advantage of a new system of doing the refresher course via computer—the 21st century way. The barrier that had stood in my way was the fact that I did not have a computer and did not know how to use one. I have been using my 15-year-old obsolete IBM word processor for letter writing, but that was all.

Fortunately for me, I have a daughter who is a whiz on computers and she gave me some necessary instructions on a new computer and then left me on my own while she flew off on a tour of Australia and New Zealand. Although she sends me e-mails of her adventures, that is a one-way street—I can't catch her in her travels to ask questions. I am writing this on my new computer and it sometimes plays tricks on me.

I received two advertisements in the mail offering computer CFI renewal courses via computer and accepted one from American Flyers (http://www.americanflyers.net). The really big surprise was the price, only $100. I accepted it with alacrity, if you know what I mean. Then I stumbled, wavered, wandered and floundered through learning how to use the new computer while taking the course—and finally won the game!

The course was great. It has a lot of thorough reading matter which can be read right from the computer screen or printed out on paper for studying. I learned a lot more from it than from classroom work, and I could do it at my leisure, now and then during several days. Three months can be spent at it if desired, whenever one gets time to devote to it.

The course is divided into six sections. After studying a section, a click will bring on the test questions. The first five sections had five questions and the sixth section had 15 questions devoted to IFR approaches with GPS. I passed all of them.

The grade percentages are given instantly after the last of the questions are answered. Then the graduation certificate is shown, which can be printed out for mailing to the FAA along with your expiring certificate and an FAA Form 8710-1. WOW! I celebrated with a drink of grape juice. Ⓜ

I learned a lot more from the computer course than from classroom work, and I could do it at my leisure, now and then during several days. Three months can be spent at it if desired, whenever one gets time to devote to it.

Through the decades...

1900 — **1910** — **1920** — **1930**

1903
1st Flight, Kitty Hawk

1910
Halley's Comet

1914-18
WWI

1927
Lindbergh's flight

1928
Pilot's License required

1905
Born Dec. 15

1910
Witnessed Curtiss flight

1923
Soloed in Jenny, at 18, after learning to fly from book

1927
Witnessed Lindbergh's takeoff, Graduated Pratt, then joined Gates Flying Circus

1928
Barnstormed with J-1, A&P #2906

1929
Barnstormed with New Standard D-25

1930 — **1940** — **1950** — **1960**

1941-45
WWII

1947
1st Bonanza delivered

1950-53
Korean War

1931
Transcontinental autogiro flight

1931-33
Airport operation

1934-35
Executive flying

1936-37
Flew 247Ds for UAL

1937-39
Test pilot Kellett

1941-43
Flew DC-2s for EAL, & Columbia test pilot

Flew DC-3s for EAL

Flew DC-4s for EAL

1952
Bought Taylorcraft

Flew DC-7s for EAL

1956
Bought 1st Bonanza, C35

Flew Constellations for EAL

1930
Marine Corps Reserve aviator

1939-40
Flew rooftop air mail operation, in autogiro, for EAL

1960 — **1970** — **1980** — **1990**

1969
Armstrong walks on Moon

1977
1st Concorde SST leaves NY

1981
1st Space Shuttle launch, Columbia

1989
Fall of Berlin Wall

Flew Lockheed L-188 Electras for EAL

Flew DC-8s for EAL, 1st jet flown

1965
Retired from EAL, 35,000 hours total flight time

Police contract flying in Bell 47 helicopter

1971
Bought Baron 56TC

1987
United Flying Octogenarians established, charter member & president

1967
Charter member of the ABS

2003
100th anniversary of Wright Bros. 1st Flight at Kitty Hawk

1990 — **2000**

1999
Bought 2nd Bonanza, V35A

2001
Retraced transcontinental flight

2002
Still flying and instrument current —39,000 hours and counting...

Epilogue

WHEN STILL A YOUNG BOY, I DECIDED TO NEVER DRINK ALCOHOL OR USE COFFEE, TOBACCO OR DRUGS, AND HAVE 100 PERCENT AVOIDED THEM, BECAUSE SINCE AGE 5, I WANTED TO BE AN AVIATOR. I HAVE ALWAYS KEPT THAT GOAL, WHILE OTHER BOYS DRIFTED ALONG WITHOUT ANY DEFINITE PLAN FOR THEIR LIVES.

To this day, I am in excellent and vigorous health and attribute that to my style of living. At age 11, I decided to cut fats from my diet because I did not wish to become fat. That gave me a headstart on most people, though we know much more about fats now than we did then.

I've always eaten a high proportion of green vegetables and fruits and avoided overeating. During the past two decades, I have avoided most red meats and concentrated instead on seafood. When I learned of the deleterious effect of the sun, I began avoiding exposure to it.

I am not an athlete but do take frequent brisk walks up and down hills. My recent physical examination showed high bone density, low cholesterol and blood pressure of 130/70. Due to my age, my height has shrunk from 6 feet 2 ½ inches to 5 feet 11 ¾ inches. My weight is 165 pounds and I have no "belly." I still have my teeth but not much hair.

Long ago I noticed that fat people and athletes do not seem to live long. I enjoy my life so much that I am happy to live a long time— I'm having so much fun. Ⓜ

"Flying is a youth preservative— if you live through it."